DISCARDED

Studies in American Popular History and Culture

Edited by
Jerome Nadelhaft

A Routledge Series

Studies in American Popular History and Culture

Jerome Nadelhaft, *General Editor*

Public Lives, Private Virtues
Images of American Revolutionary War Heroes, 1782–1832
Christopher Harris

Tales of Liberation, Strategies of Containment
Divorce and the Representation of Womanhood in American Fiction, 1880–1920
Debra Ann MacComb

Reading Comics
Language, Culture, and the Concept of the Superhero in Comic Books
Barbara A. Faggins

The Clubwomen's Daughters
Collectivist Impulses in Progressive-Era Girls' Fiction
Gwen Athene Tarbox

The Factory Girl and the Seamstress
Imagining Gender and Class in Nineteenth Century American Fiction
Amal Amireh

Writing Jazz
Race, Nationalism, and Modern Culture in the 1920s
Nicholas M. Evans

Automobility
Social Changes in the American South, 1909–1939
Corey T. Lesseig

Actors and Activists
Politics, Performance, and Exchange among Social Worlds
David A. Schlossman

Studies in the Land
The Northeast Corner
David C. Smith

First Do No Harm
Empathy and the Writing of Medical Journal Articles
Mary E. Knatterud

Piety and Power
Gender and Religious Culture in the American Colonies, 1630–1700
Leslie Lindenauer

Race-ing Masculinity
Identity in Contemporary U.S. Men's Writing
John Christopher Cunningham

Crime and the Nation
Prison Reform and Popular Fiction in Philadelphia, 1786–1800
Peter Okun

Food in Film
A Culinary Performance of Communication
Jane Ferry

Deconstructing Post-WWII New York City
The Literature, Art, Jazz, and Architecture of an Emerging Global Capital
Robert Bennett

Rethinking the Red Scare
The Lusk Committee and New York's Crusade against Radicalism, 1919–1923
Todd J. Pfannestiel

Hollywood and the Rise of Physical Culture
Heather Addison

Homelessness in American Literature
Romanticism, Realism, and Testimony
John Allen

No Way of Knowing
Crime, Urban Legends, and the Internet
Pamela Donovan

The Making of the Primitive Baptists
A Cultural and Intellectual History of the Antimission Movement, 1800–1840
James R. Mathis

WOMEN AND COMEDY IN SOLO PERFORMANCE
Phyllis Diller, Lily Tomlin and Roseanne

Suzanne Lavin

Routledge
New York & London

Published in 2004 by
Routledge
29 West 35th Street
New York, NY 10001
www.routledge-ny.com

Published in Great Britain by
Routledge
11 New Fetter Lane
London EC4P 4EE
www.routledge.co.uk

Routledge is an imprint of the Taylor & Francis Group
Printed in the United States of America on acid-free paper.

Copyright © 2004 by Taylor & Francis Books, Inc.

All rights reserved. No part of this book may be reprinted or reproduced or utilized in any form or by any electronic, mechanical, or other means, now known or hereafter invented, including photocopying and recording, or in any information storage or retrieval system, without permission in writing from the publisher.

10 9 8 7 6 5 4 3 2 1

Library of Congress Cataloging-in-Publication Data

Lavin, Suzanne, 1946-
    Women and comedy in solo performance: Phyllis Diller, Lily Tomlin, and Roseanne / by Suzanne Lavin.
      p. cm. — (Studies in American popular history and culture)
    Includes bibliographical references and index.
    ISBN 0-415-94858-4 (alk. paper)
      1. Stand-up comedy—United States. 2. Women comedians—United States—Biography I. Title. II. Series: American popular history and culture (Routledge (Firm)).
PN1969.C65L38 2004
792.7'082'0973—dc22
                                                                  2003020613

Contents

ACKNOWLEDGMENTS vii

CHAPTER ONE
Overview 1

CHAPTER TWO
Phyllis Diller
The Clown as Stand-Up Comedian 17

CHAPTER THREE
Lily Tomlin
Breaking with Tradition 33

CHAPTER FOUR
Roseanne
Fighting for Women's Comic Voice 53

CHAPTER FIVE
Women's Comedy on the Stage
The Search for Signs of Intelligent Life in the Universe, by Jane Wagner 71

CHAPTER SIX
Feminist Humor and Change
The Work of Kate Clinton, Paula Poundstone, and Whoopi Goldberg 89

CHAPTER SEVEN
Margaret Cho and Ellen DeGeneres
Directions for Women in Stand-Up   113

NOTES   131
BIBLIOGRAPHY   133
INDEX   145

Acknowledgments

I WOULD LIKE TO EXPRESS MY DEEP GRATITUDE TO JACK REAL, MY HUSBAND, who has been my great supporter and my first reader. I am grateful to my daughter, Kate Furze, and Maryann Lavin Rodgers and Mark Rodgers, my sister and her husband, all of whom gave me shelter from the storm and a safe harbor for writing. Professor Oliver Gerland of The University of Colorado at Boulder, my thesis advisor, gave me rare, steadfast, and intelligent support in guiding me through the academic waters. I want to thank Todd Horn and the Kent Denver School for its support of the Ph.D. through its generous professional development program. Finally, I am grateful to Kimberly Guinta and John Shea, my editors at Routledge, who encouraged me through all phases of this project.

Grateful acknowledgment is made for permission to reprint the following works:

> Excerpts from *The Search for Intelligent Life in the Universe* by Jane Wagner. Copyright 1987 by Jane Wagner. Reprinted by permission of Harper Collins Publishers.

> Excerpts from the "Making Light: Some Notes on Feminist Humor," unpublished essay by Kate Clinton. Reprinted by permission of Kate Clinton.

CHAPTER ONE

Overview

> The foamy wavelets curled up to her white feet, and coiled like serpents about her ankles. She walked out. The water was chill, but she walked on.... She did not look back now, but went on and on, thinking of the blue-grass meadow that she had traversed when a little child, believing it had no beginning and no end.
>
> Kate Chopin, *The Awakening* (152).

IN KATE CHOPIN'S NOVELLA *THE AWAKENING*, EDNA, THE MAIN CHARACTER, walks out into the sea, leaving behind her husband and children and all who would silence and suffocate her. Edna could no longer bear the frustration that she had something to say and no one to listen to her. By contrast, today's women solo comedy performers speak their minds to all who listen. By standing up, talking back, and acting up, they challenge society by addressing those points where it would confine and diminish them. Equipped with their intelligence and wit, they, like Hamlet, "take up arms against a sea of troubles." Their aim: "to expose and end them."

This study argues that contemporary solo comic performance by women serves as a cultural index, reflecting women's emergence as unique cultural commentators and as contemporary satirists. As women's humor continues its emergence from the privacy of the home to the public forum of the stage, it reflects realities of women's experiences, distinct from the male experiences, which have shaped the dominant tradition of stand-up. This blossoming of women's public speech in performance is as important to women's performance history and women's humor as a rainstorm after a drought. From the time of the severe cultural restrictions of the '50s and early '60s, women comedians have used their wider freedoms to reflect their changing lives. Since women were essentially barred from stand-up until Phyllis Diller's entry in the '50s, and since the period of the great growth in stand-up, the '80s, corresponds to the period of intense growth in the social status of women, women's stand-up serves as a compressed record of social change. An examination of the routines of three popular women comedians reveals a growth in the directness with which women address the sexism of their day. Phyllis Diller, for example, breaking into stand-up in 1955, took a circuitous route in addressing issues of gender inequity. Diller's content centered on the domestic arena and she played down her sensuality in order to accommodate gender restrictions. Since she wanted to appeal to a mainstream audience in clubs and on television, Diller made both her content and her stage character palatable to the socially-conservative audience of her day.

Working primarily in stand-up during the '70s and '80s, Lily Tomlin, one of the first feminist comedians, uses the momentum of the women's movement to openly address gender and class inequities. An intelligent and satirical comedian, she works primarily as a solo character performer, physically transforming herself into different characters, thus defining her approach to comedy. Tomlin's form reflects the legacy of the "New Wave" comedians of the '50s, like the team of Mike Nichols and Elaine May. Comedians like Lenny Bruce expanded stand-up from its "pure" form of one comedian telling prepared jokes, to Bruce's more relaxed and conversational stand-up, and Nichols' and May's improvised character sketches. Like Bruce and Nichols and May, Tomlin charges her comedy with social commentary.

Working primarily in the '80s and '90s, Roseanne's stand-up replaces the indirectness of the '50s with frontal assault. Like Phyllis Diller, Roseanne bases her early stand-up and her sitcom on the housewife role, but, unlike Diller, Roseanne targets men, not herself; she replaces Diller's self-deprecating style with a self-elevating style, introducing herself as a "domestic goddess." Building on the social critique employed by Lily Tomlin, Roseanne offers one form of liberation to women's comedy by demystifying feminine behavior in her use of street language, poor grammar, and unapologetic anger at patriarchal norms. The study sees these women, immensely popular with both genders, as important markers on the road of feminist solo performance comedy, a road busily under construction.

Because of the growing popularity of women's stand-up and more fertile ground for its reception, many other women took to the stage. Kate Clinton, Paula Poundstone, and Whoopi Goldberg developed comedy with a strong point of view on social issues. As one of the first comedians on the "lescom" circuit, Kate Clinton celebrated the lesbian community. Over time, her sharp political commentary occupied a greater force in her concerts. Like Clinton, Paula Poundstone also told politically barbed jokes and stories, but she appeals to the mainstream and uses domestic humor from a single mom's viewpoint. Whoopi Goldberg focuses her solo work primarily on the disenfranchised of society. Her stand-up and one-woman shows point to inequities from class, race, and gender.

As the stand-up phenomenon unfolds, women have taken advantage of different directions open to them in the field. Margaret Cho has a bawdy satiric humor in the style of Richard Pryor, with the iconoclastic edge of Roseanne. Far gentler and less satiric, Ellen DeGeneres entertains with an observational humor based on the ironies of daily life. Both tour nationally and have found loyal audiences among different groups in society. The strength of DeGeneres' comedy has helped her maintain a high profile on the stand-up stage, even though there are those who question the morality of her sexual orientation. The richness and variety of women in stand-up attests to its health, not only as a source of entertainment, but as a barometer of a dynamic culture.

METHODOLOGY

Rapid growth in women's comedy, particularly in stand-up, points to the need to find critical frames with which to examine this immensely popular performance form. Two critical frames shape this study. First, the definition of stand-up as developed by humor scholar Lawrence Mintz, and second, the work of Nancy Walker and other feminist humor scholars who have defined the contributions of feminist comedy. The work of both scholars is outlined in chapter one.

According to Mintz, women stand-up comedians who use some part of their routine to question conventional assumptions of society conform in large part with the role of stand-ups historically ("Standup" 75). Mintz discerns two social roles performed by the stand-up comedian: first, that of licensed spokesperson who "is permitted to say the things about our society that we want and need to have uttered publicly, but which would be too dangerous and too volatile if done so without the mediation of humor"; second, that of negative exemplar, the comic character who represents traits which the audience wants to "hold up to ridicule, to feel superior to, to renounce through laughter" (Mintz, "New Wave" 1).

Supporting Mintz's findings, anthropologist Stephanie Koziski Olson links the role of stand-ups with the role of clowns in that, like clowns, stand-ups "display human foibles in such a way as to connect an audience to its humanness and to act out chaotic behavior that contrasts with behavior supportive of social cohesiveness" (111). By displaying human weakness, the stand-up serves as a negative exemplar, which draws on the spectator's empathy and softens the ground for laughter. Koziski Olson shows how in ancient clowning rituals the clown appears funny—the negative exemplar role—but at the same time functions to advance the ritual and the interests of the traditional culture—the licensed spokesperson role (110).

A classic example of the negative exemplar would be the fool in Shakespeare's *King Lear*, who ridicules the king but guides him out of the storm. I argue that women solo comedy performers function somewhat like Lear's fool in their attempt to redirect the dominant culture away from its blind ways. In the hands of many women comedians, the negative exemplar role has shifted considerably through the decades, since, as women gained social freedom, many openly challenged rather than cleverly undermined the traditional culture that had oppressed them.

The work of woman humor scholar Nancy Walker helps elucidate this kind of stand-up comedy, which she defines as "feminist humor" (152). As distinct from "female humor," which, written and/or performed by women, still accepts the status quo, feminist humor works against it. "[It] assumes that women are human beings with inherent equality to men in spite of long-standing traditions and beliefs to the contrary" (152). Walker derives her definition from Gloria Kaufman's introduction to *Pulling Our Own Strings,* where Kaufman emphasizes "social revolution" as the aim of feminist humor, distinguishing it from "female" humor that works within the system from "an accepting point of view" (143). Walker's analysis of feminist humor applies to the themes that underlie much of the comedy of this study, to the extent that the humor of Phyllis Diller, Lily Tomlin, and Roseanne ridicules what Walker terms "the fundamental absurdity of one gender oppressing the other" (163). As licensed spokespersons, a license confirmed by their popularity, Diller, Tomlin, and Roseanne create comedy that exposes inequities and urges change. Likewise, those who follow in their path, Kate Clinton, Paula Poundstone, Whoopi Goldberg, Margaret Cho, and Ellen DeGeneres illuminate social injustices in their comedy.

The housewife routines of Phyllis Diller and Roseanne exemplify Walker's point. Even though she was operating under the severe cultural constraints of the '50s, Diller nonetheless attacked the idealization of women in the housewife role. By exposing herself as a complete bungler in the roles of housewife and mother, she subtly criticized the ridiculous expectations that these duties be executed perfectly. In this sense, Diller's comedy was a social critique and a call for change. Likewise, Roseanne, operating under fewer cultural restraints, ridicules many of the double standards that influenced behavior of men and women. She ridicules men, for example, for not participating equally in housework. By shifting the target from her own incompetence to those of a man, Roseanne uses comedy as a weapon of change.

Chapters two through seven recreate the cultural frame within which the comedian worked in order to determine the degree to which her comedy challenged traditional expectations for women. Underlying this portion of the analysis will be the work of anthropologist and humor scholar Mahavdev E. Apte, whose work presents the idealization of women as the chief obstacle to women's humor:

> Although women are no less capable of developing and appreciating humor than men, women have been denied similar opportunities for publicly engaging in humor. Because modesty, passivity, and virtue are associated with ideal womanhood, women have been confined to the private domain, with many constraints placed upon them (18).

Each chapter will also analyze the comic texts of each comedian to discern individual themes and style. Working within the limitation that the written text

Overview

in no way substitutes for the performance text of each comedian, this study will analyze the craft and use of language for each woman. Whenever possible, live performances, video performance, and audio performance tapes will augment the study. Interviews with the comedians have been important to the analysis, including a personal interview with Phyllis Diller.

SIGNIFICANCE OF THE STUDY

Given the immense popularity of women's stand-up, the growing body of scholarship on women and humor, and our growing understanding of the biases against women in American culture, the time is ripe for a historical study of women in solo performance. Prominent scholar Regina Barreca emphasizes the particular need for scholarship that centers on women's humor:

> We cannot underestimate the continuing need to focus on the particulars of women's comedy, humor, and in addition, women's response to men's humor. It is of particular importance to place women at the center of a discussion of comedy because it has been done too rarely even in contemporary critical studies (2).

Even though the greater critical attention to male stand-ups is understandable given the sparse attention the comedy field itself has received until recently, and the small number of women in the stand-up field until the '80s, nonetheless, there are many distinct themes in women's stand-up that offer a unique opportunity to understand further women's comedy and the changing role of women in society. Mintz suggests that stand-up needs to be studied more carefully as a cultural indicator:

> Thorough studies of joke texts and comic routines are needed as well as more careful analyses of forms and techniques. . . . Until stand-up is studied as a social phenomenon we can only speculate as to its true meaning. It is safe to say, however, that stand-up comedy in America operates within a universal tradition, both historically and across cultures, that it confronts just about all of the profoundly important aspects of our culture and society ("Standup" 80).

Contemporary stand-up serves as a rebuttal to misreadings of women's humor. Countering the dismissal of literary women humorists of the last two centuries, the scholarship of Walker, Barreca and many others helps reposition this material to highlight its feminist nature. In an even more visible way, women's stand-up requires aggression and a sense of satire, contradicting those critics who would see women's humor as weak, unprovocative, and trivial. Analysis of comic routines demonstrates that many women stand-ups are true provocateurs, who strip down society to its bare bones and point up its inequities.

Significance of the study also results from its scholarly attention to the humor field in general, and the women's humor field in particular, both long ignored or regarded with ambivalence by the scholarly community. If scholars have largely undervalued the field of humor, as Walker suggests, women's place in that field has been virtually dismissed, making the American tradition of women and humor invisible even to women (5). In addition to the work of Walker, Barreca, and Sheppard, this study builds on the research of contemporary theater scholars Elin Diamond, Sue Ellen Case, Lynda Hart, and others, and further extends work on humor into women's solo performance comedy. To further delineate and claim the tradition of women and comedy in performance, this study follows a historical timeline, which allows the current of time to push to the surface those patterns ignored in other critical analyses of American humor.

The study foregrounds the comedians' own words, and uses a large body of journalistic materials, including interviews, to discern their contributions. Roseanne Barr, Margaret Cho, Kate Clinton, Ellen DeGeneres, and Whoopi Goldberg have written books about themselves, their comedy, their themes, and their methods. In addition, each of the comedians who has written a book also has her own website, which contains valuable information from biography to performance dates. (Lily Tomlin's website raises the art up a notch.)[1] The comedians' reflections on the creation of their work and on their choice of themes have been invaluable to this study. The study also uses a relatively small body of critical work on stand-up and each comedian to shape major points. This critical work will emphasize the degree to which feminist women's stand-up reverses the traditional image of women and humor. Whereas much of women's humor has been invisible, private, and constrained by the requirements of decorum, women's stand-up is visible, public, and often openly subversive.

In order to lay the groundwork for the specific cultural context of each comedian, a brief investigation of women's socialization toward comedy is necessary. Many women who were interested in being comedians claim they were socialized against it. Not only were there few models for them, there was also social discouragement against pursuing this aggressive career. A very successful writer and performer of comedy, Maureen Gaffney, of the off-Broadway show *The Kathy and Mo Show* (1989), remembers how it felt to be a young girl in the '60s and '70s watching comedians on television:

> There were always so many male comedians, and my sisters and I would love it when the women comics would come on. All of them. Just to know it was OK for a woman to be funny, because you certainly weren't valued for that. You were valued for being pretty. . . I think you have to be really smart to be funny, at least if you're being funny on purpose (*Standing Up for Women*).

Gaffney's comment reveals a dilemma for women comedians in American culture. In valuing women's sexual attractiveness much more than their creativity or aggressiveness, the culture effectively discouraged female comedians. Psychologist Paul McPhee asserts that there is a high cost to a young woman in asserting her humor:

> Because of the power associated with the successful use of humor, humor initiation has become associated with other traditionally masculine characteristics, such as aggressiveness, dominance, and assertiveness. For a female to develop into a clown or joker, then she must violate the behavioral pattern normally reserved for women (183-4).

Female stand-ups were often rejected because they violated behavioral expectations for women. Even Johnny Carson, responsible for launching the careers of so many comedians, had difficulty as late as 1979 with female comedians: "A woman is feminine, a woman is not abrasive, a woman is not a hustler.... I think it's much tougher for women. You don't see many of them around. And the ones that try sometimes are a little aggressive for my taste. I'll take it from a guy, but from women, sometimes, it just doesn't fit too well" (qtd. in Berger 396). Given the cultural weight on a young girl against humor creation, why would she persist in generating it? Several comedians remembered that when they were young they used humor to increase their social status. Gilda Radner describes using humor to hold onto rather than give away her power to the ridiculing laughter of others. Radner claimed that as a young girl she had such a fear of being a fool that she played the fool. Her nanny, Dibby, advised her, "You laugh at yourself first before anyone else has a chance to laugh at you" (qtd. in Collier 133). Diller claims that she used humor to combat puberty:

> Becoming a comedian was my way of adjusting to puberty. When I reached that self-conscious age where I looked like Olive Oyle and wanted to look like Jean Harlow, I knew something had to be done. From twelve on, the only way to handle the terror of social situations was comedy—break the ice, make everybody laugh. I did it to make people feel more relaxed, including myself (qtd. in Collier 2).

Stockard Channing recalls how important humor was to her sense of self: "I remember that in school I was not athletic and wasn't very good at competitive sports, so I would be more of a clown. That was how I got my authority and my position" (53). By seeking power through personal humor, women not only challenge cultural restrictions, they amplify humor's already subversive nature.

A point on which many professional women comedians agree is that humor is worth creating because it is powerful. At the age of 78, Diller was still confirming the power of comedy performance: "There is no dope like laughter. Once you start creating it, you can't stop. Take Bob Hope, for instance. He's 92 years old. He can't see and he can't hear, but each morning he gets up and wants to perform" (Diller, Interview). New York comedian Susie Essman states: "I see myself as a warrior when I go out there, because comedy is a pretty aggressive act. But I also know that when I'm being my best—being myself and being funny—I've got a lot of power" (qtd. in Barreca, *Snow White* 96). For some comedians there is a great pleasure in just sharing their viewpoint. Stand-up comedian Zora Rasmussen says of her work: "It's just the world according to me. This is how I see the world, so I share that" (qtd. in Collier 20). Like other professional comedians, Gilda Radner took the risks for the benefit of expressing herself. Radner knew that she was taking risks by being funny: "Because comedy is powerful, it can seem like a threat to some people" (qtd. in Collier 138).

HISTORY

Women's stand-up is rich in satire, aggression, and freedom of expression but it emerges from a history of women's comic performance which does not share these traits. Despite the lightness by which women's comedy is labeled, its complexity demands a longer view. As women's humor scholar Alice Sheppard points out, "Historic humor enables one to rediscover perceived incongruities and thus reconstruct a lost perspective" (126). Even though its historical path was greatly shaped by the expectations of the dominant male humor, women's comedy has developed in much different ways, not only in reaction to cultural restrictions on women, but also because of the influence of race, class, and sexual preference in women's lives. Though early male and female comedians built upon comedy in which women were stereotyped, this traditional comedy was created primarily for entertainment.

By contrast, many contemporary women stand-ups have moved away from this traditional style into a comedy of social commentary, which aims in part to point out the cultural constrictions on women's lives. This social commentary not only addresses issues of the patriarchy, but, in the case of some women of color and lesbians, it addresses race and sexual preference. Assumptions that women's adult lives have to be played out as white, middle class, heterosexual standards are challenged by comedians like Whoopi Goldberg, Kate Clinton, Margaret Cho, and Ellen DeGeneres. Some contemporary comedians call for a different power structure in society, one where women's lives are not only respected equally with men's lives, but with the lives of other women. By ridiculing false assumptions of sameness, much of women's stand-up works to reinforce diversity.

The work of mainstream comedians Phyllis Diller, Lily Tomlin, and Roseanne each builds from different historical models, depending on the purpose of their comedy. Since the work of Cho, Clinton, DeGeneres, Goldberg, and Poundstone built out of the work of Diller and Tomlin particularly, it is important to understand their sources. Diller saw Bob Hope as her mentor; Tomlin was inspired by Elaine May, and Roseanne admired Lenny Bruce and Richard Pryor. Although influences on each comedian will be presented in more depth in the individual chapters, it is helpful at the onset to chronicle how comic antecedents shaped each woman's work.

Diller's model, Bob Hope, serves as a one-man history of comedy in America. Having grown up in vaudeville and having adapted his material to radio and then television, Hope was a master of the traditional routine. His solo stand-up relied on the joke with its traditional set-up, pause, and punchline. These joke routines were memorized, short, with minimal direct interaction with the audience. This persona, or stage character, was most often a version of the self-deprecating clown. Rodney Dangerfield, another traditional comedian, was not in real life a total loser whose wife cheated openly on him; rather, Dangerfield was operating within the "cuckold" style of humor that was centuries old.

Teams of comedians, like Abbott/Costello, Burns/Allen, and Martin/Lewis, also flourished in this style, one straight comedian feeding the other comedian the "set up" (the straight part of the routine), which led to the other comedian delivering the laugh line (Wilde, *Comedians* 136). This style often relies upon insult-dialogue or verbal humor (Mintz "New Wave" 2). Examining a routine of Burns and Allen not only demonstrates this traditional style, but also illuminates some of the cultural issues for women comedians in this style. Here George Burns "set up" Gracie Allen for the laugh lines:

> George: You're absolutely brilliant. I'm beginning to think you are a wizard.
> Gracie: I'm a wizard?
> George: Yes. You know what a wizard is.
> Gracie: Yes, a snowstorm.
> George: Well, if that's a snowstorm, then what's a blizzard?
> Gracie: A blizzard is the inside of a chicken (qtd. in Martin 147).

Even though Gracie Allen was one of few women from 1923–1958 recognized nationally for her humor, her comedic success was based on the stereotype of woman as scatterbrain (Martin 142–153). As seen above, her intelligence is portrayed as so limited that she mangles the language. Ironically, the team had actually reversed a typical power structure, giving Gracie dominance; usually in male/female teams, the man took the laugh line and the woman fed the straight line. Burns gave them to Gracie because he recognized that her ability to get laughs was greater than his. Burns also eliminated all lines that would make Gracie sarcastic or intelligent. "The audience didn't want her to be smart," said Burns, reflecting low cultural expectations for the intelligence of women comedians (qtd. in Martin 144).

The twentieth century pattern of women comedians perpetuating stereotypes was rarely broken until the work of Moms Mabley in the '40s and Elaine

May in the late '50s. In the nineteenth century, comedians like Lotta Crabtree had entertained in mining camps and on urban stages without the boundaries of stereotypes (38-42), but the twentieth century was dominated by limited images of women. Among the most popular stereotype has been the "dumb blonde" (100). Alternate images of women as dumb, man-chasing, and/or physically unattractive dominated women's comedy from the '20s to the late '50s. Even Fanny Brice, considered one of the most brilliant clowns in American performance history, with a career spanning 1906-1951, became best known for her song "My Man," which portrays a woman so dependent on a man that even his unfaithfulness doesn't deter her (111). Her parodies of the great dancers of the Follies—the fan dancer who couldn't open her fan or the ballet dancer who couldn't keep her balance in *The Dying Swan*—were brilliant physical comedies close to the physical comedy of slapstick. To sustain her career into her later years, Brice replaced her physical comedy with her child character Baby Snooks (Martin 115).

Of all the early female comedians, the only one who truly modeled independence was Mae West (1893-1980). Though her persona was a version of the femme fatale, she opened up sexuality as a subject for a woman character: "Too much of a good thing can be wonderful." She also showed aggressiveness as a female character: "I generally avoid temptation. Unless I can't resist it." In addition, West wrote and controlled her own material. West wrote, co-produced, and was the star of the play *Sex* (1926), and she wrote, directed, and was the star of *Diamond Lil* (1928). Even when censors cut or modified her lines, West insisted upon control of her screen work (Ward 180).

Enormously self-assured, she never apologized for who she was, and her private life reflected the sexual freedom that her characters espoused. In her plays, films and stage shows, West presented herself as an equal to men, and she was willing to go to jail for the freedom to put on her plays (180). Roseanne, known for her aggression and brashness, credits Mae West as an important influence (Barr viii).

In this short list of female comedians, one who really turned the tide for women was Elaine May, who with Mike Nichols created a satiric and substantial comedy which ushered in a new era in improvisation and stand-up. As I will indicate later in my discussion of Lily Tomlin, Elaine May demonstrates what a woman comedian could become if she were free of cultural stereotypes. She was a complete equal in the improvisational act she did with Mike Nichols, in which they fiercely satirized middle class complacency and pointed out its hypocrisies. A Nichols and May routine on funeral scams, for example, won the hostility of undertakers throughout the country for its tone toward the industry's shameless profiteering:

> May: Welcome to Lawn Dust. Can I help you?
> Nichols: Yes. I've read your ad. I'm interested in the $85.00 funeral.
> May: Was that for yourself?

Nichols: No.
May: May I ask, where did you catch our ad?
Nichols: TV Guide.
May: I am your grief lady, Miss Loomis. . . . That will be $85.00.
Nichols: (giving her the money) I have the check all made out.
May: Before you go, would you be interested in any extras?
Nichols: What kind of extras?
May: Well, how about a casket? (Nichols and May)

Nichols and May were contemporaries of Mort Sahl and Lenny Bruce. Considered "New Wave" comedians, they changed the face of traditional comedy by injecting it with realistic observation to a degree foreign to the benign humor of the '50s and '60s. Breaking away from sole dependence on the punchline joke, they told stories, became characters, or shared their observations. Their humor lived in the real world and challenged its consciousness (Mintz, "Standup" 2). Termed "New Wave" comedians because of these differences in style and content, they used humor to examine society.

Lenny Bruce, for example, assailed hypocrisies and presented paradoxes that exposed moral bankruptcy: "The smoking of marijuana should be encouraged because it does not induce lung cancer. Children ought to watch pornographic movies: it's healthier than learning about sex from Hollywood" (qtd. in Tynan xii). Bruce was challenged, attacked, and arrested for his performances in which he talked freely of sex, drugs, and religion, used street language, and openly confronted middle class conformity (Berger 74–88):

Show me the average sex maniac, the one who takes your eight-year-old, *schtupps* her in the parking lot, and then kills her, and I'll show you a guy who's had a good religious upbringing. You see, he saw his father or mother always telling his sister to cover up her body, when she was only six years old, and so he figured, one day I'm going to find out what it is she's covering, and if it's as dirty as my father says I'll kill it (qtd. in Allen 76-7).

Contrast this brand of ironic observation with the straightforward comedy of the following mother-in-law joke of the '50s and '60s-style comedian, Henny Youngman: "I'm here on a pleasure trip. I took my mother-in-law to the airport" (qtd. in Young).

Also exemplary is the following wife joke of another comedian of that era, Jackie Vernon: "My wife, Blossom, died of bon-bon poisoning. I cremated her and mixed her with marijuana. That's the best that shit made me feel" (qtd. in Young). Apart from the obvious contrast in form, observation versus the joke, there is a starting contrast in the perception of reality. Undergirding the wife jokes of Youngman and Vernon is the belief in comedy primarily as entertainment and escape; it reinforces the status quo. Youngman and Vernon easily use insult humor to put their audience at ease and to set up their innocent world. Undergirding

Lenny Bruce's world is the belief that political and social reality needs to be reexamined for the contradictions between perceived truth and actual truth. Bruce confronted a social system that showed moral outrage at the use of the word "fuck," but endorsed the death penalty (Tynan x).

In "New Wave" comedy, humor could be used to expose corruption, as did Nichols' and May's, or as a weapon to combat injustice, as Dick Gregory's comedy did. The following routine by Gregory exemplifies not only a form different from the traditional pattern, but also a rejection in content of the status quo:

> About that time these three cousins come in, you know the ones I mean, Ku, Klux, and Klan, and they say, "Boy, we're givin' you fair warnin'. Anything you do to that chicken, we're gonna do to you."... So I put down my knife and fork, and I picked up that chicken, and I *kissed* it (qtd. in Wilde, *Comedians* 250).

Likewise, this routine of Nichols and May challenges the money machine of Hollywood and the pitiful programming of television:

> Ladies and gentlemen, I am proud to be able to present the following award.... There will be a lot said here tonight about excellence and the creative, the artistic ... but what of the others in this industry? Seriously, there are men in the industry who go on, year in and year out, quietly and unassumingly, producing garbage. I am very, very proud to be chosen by the academy to present tonight's special award to the man who has been voted: "The Most Total Mediocrity" in the industry, [lights up on Nichols] (qtd. in Nichols and May).

These comedians aimed to increase audience awareness of trends that were fracturing the culture. Thus, they shifted the emphasis of comedy from entertainment to a sociopolitical commentary. This reverses an earlier pattern in theater history when the biting satire of Aristophanes gave way to the romantic escapism of Menander.

In addition to opening up subject matter of stand-up, the "New Wave" comedians opened up the style. Nichols and May were improvisational character comedians, dependent upon a bright verbal and physical comedy, which was interactive with the audience and unmemorized. They ended their 1960 Broadway show with a skit built around a first and last line provided by the audience (Nichols and May). Lenny Bruce created his humor from his own observations, and his stand-up was sharing what he observed. Routines were deliberately not memorized:

> When I talk on the stage, people often have the impression that I make up things as I go along. This isn't true. I know a lot of things I want to say; I'm just not exactly sure when I will say them. This process of allowing one sub-

> ject spontaneously to free associate with another is equivalent to James
> Joyce's stream of consciousness (Bruce 44).

Kenneth Tynan called Bruce "an impromptu prose poet who trusted his audience so completely that he could talk in public no less outspokenly than he would talk in private" (xii). This easy relationship with the audience emphasized an informality. Bruce did not have an elaborate stage persona. Rather, he heightened his own philosophical and intellectual reflections for his public performances. Tynan describes the effect of Bruce's style: "By the end of the evening he had crashed through frontiers of language and feeling that I had hitherto thought impregnable" (xii).

These differences in style and material represented by Nichols and May and Lenny Bruce would affect women comedians after them, particularly those like Lily Tomlin who did character comedy rather than traditional stand-up. Because of the range of comic styles introduced into stand-up after Lenny Bruce, Lawrence Mintz argues for a wider definition of stand-up which is not limited to the one comic in direct address telling jokes: "We must therefore broaden our scope at least to include seated storytellers, comic characterizations that employ costume and prop, team acts…skits, and improvisational situations" (Mintz, "Standup" 71). The "New Wave" comedians developed new venues, often working in folk music houses, coffee houses, and college auditoriums (Mintz, "New Wave" 2). They dressed casually and developed humor from comic situations, rather than using the joke form (2). Their social satire recalled Mark Twain, Artemeus Ward, or Will Rogers more than Jack Benny or Bob Hope (2). Since the "New Wave" comedians were dependent upon observation of the shifting political and social scene, they were more open than traditional comedians to the views of women in a changing world.

I have chosen three women comedians, Phyllis Diller, Lily Tomlin, and Roseanne, to outline the shape of this new comedy as it affected women comedians. As the first woman stand-up, Diller stands as the progenitress of a long line of women solo performers in the second half of the twentieth century. By her commitment to a satirical content, Lily Tomlin significantly shifts the shape of women's solo performance away from pure entertainment to comedy that calls for social and political change. Because of her feminist commitment to change the lives of women, particularly working class women, Roseanne became one of the most important American comedians in the period from 1986 to 1996. Although many other women comedians also emerged in this period, Roseanne's brash persona and her immense popularity significantly advanced both the visibility and the sense of possibility for women comedians.

The outline of women's comedy begins to fill out in the works of Kate Clinton, Paula Poundstone, and Whoopi Goldberg who each manifest a satiric thrust. Finally the study looks at the work of Margaret Cho and Ellen DeGeneres, two popular women comedians who take advantage of the new freedom for women in stand-up to head their comedy in opposite directions.

OUTLINE

The image of women standing alone in the lights of a stage and humorously commenting on their culture is an image of women standing up for themselves. While many of the concerns of women's stand-up remain fairly constant, a shifting social consciousness heightening women's issues brought about parallel changes in women's stand-up.

Chapter One positions women's stand-up as a complex and dynamic cultural force that moves subtly through the crests and troughs of a churning culture. I use "churning" advisedly, because the rise of women's stand-up historically corresponds with one of the most revolutionary periods in the lives of women in the history of America. As each succeeding decade brings important change in women's lives, women comedians significantly shift the way they play out their roles as negative exemplars and licensed spokespersons. This study assesses these shifts as a way of reading the culture, reading women's lives, and reading women's stand-up performance.

Chapter Two shows how Phyllis Diller hammered her stand-up out of the hard rock of the mid '50s and early '60s, a time when rigid images of the "ideal woman" dominated cultural consciousness, strictly binding women to standards of unrealistic perfection as mothers, wives, and homemakers. Herself a wife and mother, Diller fabricated a stage family and cast herself as their incompetent maternal figure. As she made fun of all the engrained family roles, Diller's independent, aggressive, and bold presence was itself a stance against this suffocating iconography. Her command of the traditional punchline form and her masterful delivery made her not only competitive with male comics, but one of America's great clowns.

Chapter Three tracks the emergence of the Tomlin's comedy out of the political turbulence of the '60s and '70s, and shows how she was influenced by the Women's Movement. By expanding images of women on the stage from the housewife/mother role to broader roles which include working women, religious women, physically challenged, and homeless women, Tomlin and her collaborator, Jane Wagner, repositioned women's comedy to include feminist concerns and social and political commentary. Tomlin's work also features portraits of men, providing a window from which to see their point of view. Because Tomlin works in character comedy rather than joke telling, she shifts the role of comedian from that of negative exemplar "loser" to that of comedian as visionary and healer.

Chapter Four focuses on the work of Roseanne, one of the many women whose comedy benefited from both the models of Diller and Tomlin and from the advances made by the Women's Movement. As a negative exemplar, Roseanne refuses to play the victim/loser and plays rather victor/fighter. As a licensed spokesperson, Roseanne's housewife role challenges domestic cultural codes, and her persona shows the power of women in private life. By pushing boundaries for women in comedy to such a great degree, Roseanne not only invigorates domestic comedy, she popularly repositions it. The final section of the Roseanne chapter examines her work in her long-running sitcom, *Roseanne!* Behind the scenes of that show, Roseanne becomes a warrior for a respectful and realistic depiction of her working class characters.

Chapter Five analyzes Jane Wagner's one-woman show, written for Lily Tomlin, *The Search for Signs of Intelligent Life in the Universe*, and analyzes the play as an example of the quality of women's solo comedy that can evolve in a world where women's comedy becomes increasingly unrestricted. The study focuses on the depth of the sociopolitical commentary contained in this work.

Chapter Six takes a detailed look at the way comedy by women highlights social change. An examination of the work of Kate Clinton reveals a comedian who plays primarily to lesbian audiences and whose political critique exposes the hypocrisies of government and religion. Following Clinton, I look at the work of Paula Poundstone, equally satiric in her criticism of government, but a comedian who has a significant domestic content in her work. However, she represents a new image of a mother, single and working. Finally, this chapter examines the solo work of Whoopi Goldberg, showing her compassion for those on the fringes of society, those left out of the patriarchy. Her one-woman show *Whoopi Goldberg* introduces a group of six characters, unfamiliar to most of the audience, whom Whoopi sympathetically embodies to reveal their full humanity. I also look at her politically charged one-woman HBO show *Chez Whoopi*, which was filmed in a largely African American neighborhood in L.A. Because she can communicate to so many segments of American society with a striking honesty and a keen social conscience, Goldberg is positioned as one of the most important comedians in this study.

Chapter Seven explores the work of Margaret Cho and Ellen DeGeneres. Both women are immensely popular, but for different reasons. Those contrasts provide points on a continuum with which to view new directions for women and comedy. On the one hand, Cho appeals to an audience who enjoys her iconoclastic derision of the dominant culture, especially its shallow values regarding sexual orientation, race, and gender. On the other hand, DeGeneres maintains a broad appeal because of her ability to charm an audience with simple but important observations on everyday life. Chapter seven also explores the background and consequences of DeGeneres' decision in 1997 to have both herself and her television character on the *Ellen* show come out as gay.

Chapter Seven also looks at the effect mainstream television has had on female comedians, and they on it. The examination reveals the importance of the '80s and '90s in television for highlighting the work of stand-ups. The study examines shows of Roseanne, Margaret Cho, Brett Butler, and Ellen DeGeneres. Finally, the conclusion reviews the progress of women and comedy through its brief lifetime. While the historical timeline bends and curves, it moves steadily and stronger as an accumulating expression of the fullness, diversity, and complexity of women's voices and women's lives.

Chapter Two

Phyllis Diller

The Clown as Stand-Up Comedian

IT IS 1955. AS YOU SIT IN THE FAMOUS SAN FRANCISCO NIGHTCLUB THE PURPLE Onion, you wonder about this unknown woman about to take the stage. This is strange: women do not do stand-up comedy. She's pretty ordinary looking, a housewife you'd guess. She starts getting some laughs and you lean forward:

> I stuffed a turkey. And that's the last. It took me three weeks. Stuffed it through the beak. It was the only thing open. I was very patient. I sat there with this [sic] dinky little tweezers, while Thanksgiving went past. So then I decided to shoot for Christmas, and then I got thinking about the cheese. And we don't have room in that refrigerator for two pets. Because my ironing is in there. ... All our kids are grown and I've got baby clothes in there (*Are You Ready for Phyllis Diller?*).

You decide to stay for the second set to see if she sustains the momentum. This time she starts in on her husband, Fang: "On our honeymoon, Fang brought a book to bed. I wouldn't mind if he had read. He colored." Every joke makes you laugh and your laughter builds with the laughter of the crowd. "Fang brought home a dozen flowers. Three bottles of Four Roses." "Once I fed a stray dog and he never left. He couldn't move" (qtd. in Wilde, *Comedians* 208–9).

The Purple Onion extended Diller's initial two-week contract in 1955 to eighty-nine weeks, and in 1996, at the age of 78, when asked if she was still working, she answered, "Every day!" (Diller, Interview). An only child, born on July 17, 1917, in Lima, Ohio, to a secure and comfortable family, Phyllis Driver had time alone with her imagination. When her dad went to check on his farm in Ohio, Diller says, "I stood in the barn and sang opera to the sheep. I made up all sorts of languages. I guess someone looking in might have predicted I would grow up to be funny" (Barovick). She married Sherwood Diller in 1939, and the couple soon moved to California where she began what she hoped would be a normal family life, raising her five children. "I intended to be a housewife and a mother and the funniest woman on my block, but things changed" (*Standing Up for Women*). The realization that she had married a man who could not make a living served as catalyst for Diller to carve a strong career line. When the inheritance from her parents ran out and her family faced foreclosure and bankruptcy, Diller went to work (*Standing Up for Women*).

Diller credits a book, *The Magic of Believing* by Claude Bristol, with changing her life. She told Harriet Barovick of *Time* that "If I hadn't read it, I don't think I would have made it—the book was that important—because it outlined a system of thought that was the absolute turning point in my life, in my attitude toward myself." Before Diller read the book she felt that she had no confidence, and she didn't realize that she had talent, even though her husband had urged her to try comedy. After reading the book, Diller volunteered her comedy for church groups, PTA meetings, the Kiwanis Club, and The Red Cross, until at the age of thirty-seven, Diller made her Purple Onion debut. Personally she paid a high price to become a comedian: "There is no motivation like a mother with her young. Nothing was going to stop me. I had to get them an education and a home.... I had to give up my house, my kids went to live with their relatives and I went on the road with no home" (qtd. in Collier 6).

Once successful at The Purple Onion, Diller set a five year goal to play San Francisco's famous Hungry i comedy club. By mid 1961, much sooner than anticipated, she had not only played the Hungry i, but she had also appeared on *The Jack Paar Show* some thirty times (*Current Biography 1967*). Because of these early television appearances, Diller credits Paar with actually launching her career (Diller, Interview). As a frequent guest on leading '60s variety and comedy shows such as those of Ed Sullivan, Red Skelton, Andy Williams, Dean Martin, Steve Lawrence, and Jack Benny, Diller attracted her popular following and was soon making up to a million dollars a year (Martin 344).

In addition to her stand-up career, Diller has to her credit a television series, several records, movies, books, and overseas tours with Bob Hope (Unterbrink 86). From 1966 until the fall of 1967, ABC aired her series *The Pruitts of Southampton,* which became *The Phyllis Diller Show*. Phyllis Diller made her screen debut in *Splendor in the Grass* in 1961. Diller acted in sixteen movies, including *Boy Did I Get a Wrong Number* (1966) and several with Bob Hope such as *Eight On The Lam* (1967). In 1998 she was the voice of the queen in the animated film, *A Bug's Life* (Biography Resource Center). Her comedy records include: *Phyllis Diller Laughs* (1961); *Are You Ready for Phyllis Diller?* (1962); and *Born to Sing* (1968). Diller has four books to her credit, *Phyllis Diller's Housekeeping Hints* (1966), *Phyllis Diller's Marriage Manual* (1967), *The Complete Mother* (1969), and *The Joys of Aging and How to Avoid Them* (1981) (*Current Biography* 1967).

Diller also starred in significant roles on stage, when in 1970 she played Dolly Gallagher Levi in *Hello, Dolly!* on Broadway, and in 1988 when she played Mother Superior in *Nunsense* in San Francisco. According to the *St. James Encyclopedia of Popular Culture*, Diller has been a significant humanitarian throughout her career. In 1990 she won the Living Legend Award from The Women's International Center. She is the recipient of the "Humanitarian Award" from the AMC Cancer Research Center. She was inducted in the Women's Hall of Fame for her contribution as entertainer, author, and actress.

Diller's talents extend into the arts of music and visual art. As a teenager she spent three years training in classical piano (Barovick), and from 1971 to 1982, she played classical piano with over a hundred different symphony orchestras around the country. Using the stage name Illya Dillya she played in Detroit, Cincinnati, Houston, Denver, and many other cities, and to the surprise of the audiences, the music was serious and she earned good reviews. Diller is also a painter, and her paintings have earned up to $5,000 (Barovick). In retirement she plans to devote more time to her other arts, especially painting.

In 2002 at the age of eighty-four, Diller announced that after forty-seven years, she would retire from her stand-up career. Diller plans to continue her charity work, and to do guest appearances, but she won't change her mind about her stand-up work. With typical feistiness, she told Bob Thomas of the Associated Press, "I consider comebacks cheap. And in bad taste." When a mic failed in Palm Beach, FL, she decided that was the end of a long road of stand-up (Thomas). The *San Francisco Chronicle* reported in April 2002 that fans from all over Southern California traveled to California State University, Northridge to catch her forty-minute act, her last live stand-up performance. Said Diller, "It isn't as easy at it looks."

A significant legacy of Diller's stand-up will be the positive impact she had on young women who dreamed of being comedians. Kathy Kinney, who plays Mimi on *The Drew Carey Show,* said of Diller's inspiration: "I used to watch her whenever she was on television…. I was fascinated by her timing, her laugh, her look; at a time when most women tried to be beautiful, she just said, 'I'm just gonna look this way and be funny'" (qtd. in Thomas). Diller appeared on *The Drew Carey Show* on May 8, 2003.

A CRITICAL FRAMEWORK

Phyllis Diller's work in her long and successful career fits into the classic role of the stand-up as defined by Mintz. In her act, Diller functions as both the negative exemplar, who holds oneself up for ridicule, and the licensed spokesperson, who says what society wants or needs to have said, but who "gets away with it" through humor (Mintz, "New Wave" 1). Against the odds of the conservative '50s, Diller negotiated both roles to become a successful mainstream comic. By reducing her appearance of power, Diller's stage character, a highly exaggerated loser clown type, helped the performer confront audience resistance to a woman assuming the aggressive position of solo comedic entertainer. From her inglorious position as loser, Diller could be more effective in her second classic stand-up role, licensed spokesperson.

I argue for the importance of Phyllis Diller's comedy as a force in challenging the idealization of women as objects of beauty, happy homemakers, and unquestioning supporters of their husbands. As pointed out by scholars Apte, Walker, and others, the idealization of women was a major obstacle to women's full expression of humor, and Diller's challenge to this image helped clear the path for other women comedians. Diller's work was created from the tension between overt social pressure on women to conform to these standards of behavior, and the equally strong covert counter-pressure to break free from those unrealistic expectations. Rather than read her self-deprecating humor as a sell-out to the patriarchal culture, I argue that in its time it was a successful strategy of negotiation with that culture. Diller's stand-up broke the code of expected behavior for women by comically modeling ugliness and domestic incompetence against idealized standards of beauty and domestic perfection. Artistically, Diller's routines modeled a high degree of verbal skill both in the structure of each joke and the structure of the whole act. In content and form, Diller's pioneering work won her a large following and set a high standard for others.

Like other women literary domestic humorists of her time—Betty MacDonald with *The Egg and I* (1945), Shirley Jackson with *Life Among the Savages* (1953), and Jean Kerr with *Please Don't Eat the Daisies* (1957)—Diller's comedy ridicules specific absurdities in domestic life (Walker ix, x). In this sense, her themes fit those discerned by Nancy Walker as central to women's comedy: "the desire to claim autonomy and power" (4). Though masked, Diller's claim for more independence for women is not muted.

PHYLLIS DILLER AS NEGATIVE EXEMPLAR

Phyllis Diller played out the role of stand-up as negative exemplar (negative model) by creating a grotesque physical persona and telling jokes which turned on self-deprecation. As a clown free from the pressures of physical beauty, she could make jokes at the expense of her body. "You know why this dress looks so wild and live? It's a skin graft" (qtd. in Wilde, *Comedians* 208). Following "the loser" clown tradition, Diller also deviated from standards of conventional behavior for women, introducing herself as an incompetent housewife and mother:

> — I'm nine years behind on my ironing, I bury it in the backyard. (qtd. in Martin 338)
> — I'd do my ironing but I can't find the refrigerator. (qtd. in Wilde, *Comedians* 209)

Phyllis Diller

Through this strategy, Diller used her negative exemplar role to overshadow her dubious role as woman comedian, and thus won audience acceptance. In this respect she drew on the power of the ritualistic clown as summarized by Seymour and Rhoda Fisher:

> . . . a powerful figure whose role is to act out the idea of violating taboos. In his eccentricity and disregard of convention he portrays the deviant who dares to do what is forbidden. He dares to do the crazy, unthinkable thing. But at the same time, he presents himself as ugly, strange, and debased. There is a self-deprecatory quality in his appearance that is obviously expiatory. Thus, he is the violator of taboos but he is also clearly the "no good" one for doing so. His ugly singularity is a badge of his guilt and he is an easy target for the group to ridicule (49).

More specifically, Diller created a wildly exaggerated persona to keep the focus on the clown and away from her violation of the taboo that women could not perform stand-up.

The extent of her commitment to the negative exemplar becomes clear when one compares Diller's jokes to those of her male contemporaries, Bob Hope and Joey Bishop. As the following comparisons show, the content of these short one-liners is almost indistinguishable from Hope to Diller and from Bishop to Diller. All the jokes turn on self-deprecation:

BOB HOPE

> — I used to be quite an athlete—big chest, hard stomach. But that's all behind me now.
> — There's a dangerous side to honorary doctorates. The last time I was sick I took two aspirins and called myself in the morning (qtd. in Wilde, *Comedians* 268-9).

PHYLLIS DILLER

> — Most people get a reservation at a beauty ranch, I was committed.
> — I was arrested for taking a four-way cold tablet on a one-way street (208-9).

The following comparison of Diller's jokes with Joey Bishop's shows that economical form and self-deprecating content characterize both sets of jokes.

JOEY BISHOP

> — I was in *The Naked and the Dead*. I played both parts.
> — In my new movie, I play the part of a psychoneurotic Robin Hood. I steal from the rich, but I keep it (99-100).

Phyllis Diller

> — I never made *Who's Who* but I'm featured in *What's That*.
> — I made up my mind to show the world—and they're afraid to look
> (208-9).

Because of their similarity, the jokes help isolate gender questions regarding Diller's comedy. While the men tell their jokes in plain suits, Diller tells hers in a complicated costume. To be heard at all in the male field of stand-up, Diller had to invent a disguise to diminish her gender and she had to fit into the dominant comedy style of self-deprecation that would diminish her aggressiveness.

Diller's stage character had to be outlandish enough to overcome audience resistance, sometimes expressed in anger, at a woman doing stand-up (Martin 343). An example of the low regard attributed to daring women in the late '50s is this remark from a *Ladies Home Journal* editor: "If we get an article about a woman who does anything adventurous, out of the way, something by herself, you know, we figure she must be terribly aggressive, neurotic" (qtd. in Manchester 761). In addition to regarding female aggressiveness as neurotic, the '50s ossified gender roles by valorizing the roles of wife and mother, so that by the end of the decade the average woman was married before she was twenty and the birth rate was soaring (Hymowitz 326). Within this ethos, Diller rose to popularity only when her persona sufficiently hid her attractiveness and her level of self-deprecation sufficiently hid her aggressiveness.

Turning these cultural restrictions to her advantage, Diller developed a stage character that would not only identify her, but which would make her unforgettable. The album cover of *Born to Sing* pictures Diller standing in the middle of a chaotic kitchen, wearing pink curlers, a white feather boa, diamond necklace, white gloves, and cigarette holder, while in the background her son, gagged and tied to a kitchen chair, struggles to break free. Overhead the cat swings from the birdcage and in front of her a shirt burns as it sits on an ironing board laden with a half eaten apple and a headless chicken. This outrageous persona became her calling card.

In creating her stage identity, Diller crossed a minefield. While she couldn't be too aggressive or too beautiful, she couldn't be herself either. The very theatricality of her solo position on stage demanded a commanding persona. She learned at the very beginning of her career that it worked best for her to present a heightened character in order to sustain audience interest: "Back then I was sweet. I was too sweet" (qtd. in Collier 3). When she first started playing small jobs and clubs, she did not have a stage character.

> At first, nothing seemed to work. I was a normal looking woman—dark brown hair, wearing perfectly normal clothes that I bought off the racks—and I'd come out and try to be funny. The audience thought I was the lady down the street, which is exactly what I was. ... A guy whose club I worked in and who

knew a bit about comedy said, "You smile too much. Be hostile" (qtd. in Collier 3).

Diller claims that she invented the shapeless garment to cover her body up and to keep attention on the comedy. "I had a perfect figure. If I went out there like that, men would only see my boobs" (Diller, Interview). Over time, Diller developed a distinct physical persona, gradually presenting herself in wild dresses, fright wigs, shaved eyebrows, false eyelashes, and ankle boots. "I realized I had to lighten my hair; I needed clothes; you need to come from a strong place" (qtd. in *Standing Up for Women*).

Inventing a recognizable persona is one of the most important tasks for a new comedian, suggests Diller: "New comics must find a persona—one immediately understood by the audience, the quicker the better" (qtd. in *Standing Up for Women*). To mark her identity, Diller dressed for each occasion, making a strong visual first impression and typically using it to get her first joke, as in this excerpt from Bob Hope's Viet Nam tour. Diller enters the stage running, looking very lost in a pea green dress, wild wig, and army boots:

> It's such a thrill to be here. The only thing, it's so nerve racking. I've been captured and released twice by both sides. Bob, I have only one complaint. When we arrived here all the other girls were given large bouquets.
> BOB HOPE
> What did they give you?
> DILLER
> A machete and a map of the jungle (*Bob Hope's Overseas Christmas*).

Adding to her physical persona, she perfected her signature laugh, a raucous, "Ha, ha, ha," to punctuate key lines and to encourage audience laughter: "priming the pump," she called it (*Standing Up for Women*). Her cigarette holder also added to her timing. Like a clown's scepter, she carried it everywhere, tapping the unlit cigarette to punctuate key lines (Wilde, *Comedians* 215).

Some feminist critics have had difficulty with Diller's self-deprecation. Anne Beatts, a respected humor writer and former writer for *Saturday Night Live*, sees Diller as a poor model. "Women are allowed to be pretty and charming, but not intelligent, funny, or clever. There's always that choice; should I be Phyllis Diller and be ugly but make them laugh, or should I be beautiful and keep my mouth shut?" (qtd. in Collier 32). Beatts' comment fails to acknowledge the importance to women comedians of using the dominant humor style, self-deprecation. This excerpt from Karen M. Stoddard harshly criticizes early women stand-ups for using this humor style: "Women comics of the mid and late 1960s were imitating male comics in style and defeating themselves and other women in their choices of material" (12). Such an analysis of the early women stand-ups is like criticizing Amelia Earhart for learning to fly from a man. Comedians like Phyllis Diller and Gracie Allen are not negative models in their ugliness or self-deprecation. These women are positive models because they made full use of their intelligence to find a style of humor which would allow them visibility and presence in an era when funny women were virtually invisible or completely absent.

Placing Diller's comedy in its historical perspective allows us to shift emphasis from content to style. Diller's era of traditional comedy specialized in wife jokes and self-deprecation. Jack Benny developed a persona largely based on his stinginess (Slide 31–5). Milton Berle, a contemporary of Diller's in the '50s, laced his monologues with self-deprecating remarks:

— I just got back from Florida. I flew in. Boy, are my arms tired!
— I had a wonderful compartment of the train on the way down. But the conductor kept locking me in (qtd. in Wilde, *Comedians* 56).

Rodney Dangerfield capitalized on this style of humor well into the '80s with his "No Respect" routines:

— When I was born the doctor told my mother:
"I did what I could but he pulled through anyway."
— Every time I go into the elevator, the operator says the same thing:
"Basement?" (*Rodney Dangerfield*).

As a strong style which had characterized many of the comedy acts of vaudeville and early radio and television, acts such as Burns and Allen, Milton Berle, Jack Benny, Bob Hope, and Jerry Lewis (Wilde 36, 56–7, 132–4, 268–9, 321), self-deprecation provided Diller with a way to showcase her genuine talent. Through it she was able to do comedy without threatening women's sexual roles or men's dominance.

Under her guise as negative exemplar, Diller said things that needed to be said about the lives of women. The relationship Diller established between her "crazy" stage character and her "wise" commentary follows closely the same relationship established by classic clowns. As Towsen suggests, clowns establish "feelings of superiority in the spectator" (206). By making fun of herself Diller established an easy atmosphere for laughter, and thus was able to comment as a licensed spokesperson.

PHYLLIS DILLER AS LICENSED SPOKESPERSON

Though Diller de-emphasized gender in her stand-up function as negative exemplar, she emphasized her experience as a woman in her role as licensed spokesperson. In this way, her comedy challenged strained roles for women in the '50s and '60s. "My most avid fans were women. I was saying things about kids, husbands, mothers-in-law, things that they wanted to say but couldn't" (qtd. in

Collier 4). Ugly, messy, and grotesque, Diller exposed the drudgery of housekeeping, the headache of raising children, and the trial of being a wife.

With this recognizable loser as the base of her comedy, Phyllis Diller could develop her role as licensed spokesperson with great freedom. "I would come out on stage and put everybody down—myself, the children, the lady next door, the cops. Everybody has got to be bad" (qtd. in Collier 4). Her main target was her imaginary husband, Fang, but his mother, Moby Dick, and his loose sister, Captain Bligh, also came in for attack. Even though Sherwood Diller's mother and sister insisted after the Dillers' divorce that Phyllis Diller drop these two characters from her act, Phyllis Diller eventually sued them to keep the characters in (Martin 342). "My act is a cartoon strip; I invented everyone" (*Standing Up for Women*).

Although Diller has said that because of her gender, subjects outside private life were off limits to her (*Women of the Night*), she seized the opportunity to claim the domestic sphere as fertile comic ground. "It took me several years to find the housewife thing, talk about what I knew about, and it's lucky I had something to bitch about" (qtd. in *Standing Up for Women*). A clever strategist, Diller attracted women to her comedy by debunking the impossible ideal by which was held up to them as model.

By the standards of today, the limits on women's lives in the '50s and '60s were unimaginable. Diller's routines exposed not only their absurdity, but their suffocating effect. In the post war economy, Rosie the Riveter was asked to leave the war factory and go home. Summarized by Naomi Weisstein as "those detergent, lying, tight-ass, repressive, apolitical years" (qtd. in Hymowitz 131), the '50s were arguably the worst possible decade for a woman to break into stand-up comedy. As a mark of the social conservatism of the era, by the end of the '50s, sixty percent of all college women were dropping out to marry before they had earned a degree (326). Betty Freidan's *The Feminine Mystique* surveys contemporary women's magazines *(McCall's, Life,* and *Ladies Home Journal)* and finds women described as: "young and frivolous, almost childlike; fluffy and feminine, passive; gaily content in a world of bedroom and kitchen, sex, babies, and home" (30).

An intelligent and aware comedian, Phyllis Diller found a comic playground in the excesses of her era. Her routines typically targeted: 1) rigidity in standards of female beauty, 2) the limiting role of housewife, and 3) the dominance of men. In each of the following routines, Diller ridicules social values that artificially confine women.

DILLER ON STANDARDS OF FEMALE BEAUTY

In her early routines, Diller used *Mademoiselle* magazine and its strict standards of formal female beauty as a target. In this piece, Diller comes on the stage wearing a floor-length metallic dress. The ridiculous costume reveals her to be a hopeless failure at the "Jackie look:"

> You ready for the new look? This is it. It's a cross between Jackie Kennedy and Camelot. I haven't had a single drink and my dress is stiff. Do you know I'm the only woman in the world who gets dresses rejected by the Salvation Army? They send them back with ugly notes. With things like, "Dear Phyllis Diller, this dress could wreck a girl's life." Well, depending where she wears it. Seriously, I have a tinsmith inside, repairing it (*Phyllis Diller Laughs*).

This routine exemplifies the pattern where Diller first places herself as the butt of the joke but then challenges a social trend, in this case female mimicry of ridiculous fashions. In her "Lipstick" routine Diller shows the ridiculous results of blindly following the dictates of fashion, since she is nearly mistaken for dead as a result of wearing too light a shade of lipstick. Diller is the butt of the joke, but she lifts the consequences of her fashion mistake to a life-and-death level, thus revealing its actual triviality:

> Right now lipstick is the most important thing in the fashion picture.... You know, the new "pale" look. You look like you just might be passing on. Oh, the first time I wore it, I was followed by a mortician. But you know what really bothered me, the vultures. Because THEY know. And on top of that, I suffered a couple of direct hits. In fact, that's why I gave up saving. I couldn't get past the pigeons at the bank. It was either close the account or marry a cleaner (*Phyllis Diller Laughs*).

Another favorite beauty target is the woman who tries too hard to stay young. In this routine she describes a friend who has had plastic surgery. Diller imitates her lisp and slurred speech as the friend accidentally meets an acquaintance on the street. After making several jokes at the expense of the surgeon, Diller describes the lunch she shared with her marred friend, imitating her disrupted speech pattern whenever the friend speaks:

> We went to lunch. I couldn't eat. You wouldn't believe what happens when she chews. [pause] Nothing hits. And she's got food all down this side. We moved three times. [pause] The table kept filling up.... She said, "Phyllis, do you think this will hurt my career?" I couldn't think of a single career it wouldn't hurt. I said, "What do you do?" She said, "I'm a lipstick model" (*Phyllis Diller Laughs*).

In all of these routines Diller challenges women's complicity in their restrictions. Underlying each routine is the question, "Why are you going to these extremes?" The same question underlies Diller's routines in the limiting role of housewife.

DILLER ON THE HOUSEWIFE ROLE

Diller's debunking of the housewife role had an even wider appeal to both men and women. Television, just entering the American home in the '50s, had cast a spell where model families like the Nelsons in *Ozzie and Harriet* and the Cleavers in *Leave it to Beaver* led harmonious lives in sparkling kitchens and orderly living rooms. Ads between these shows featured grateful women rejoicing at a new dish soap or floor care product. Against this sanctified ideal, Diller established her slobbish habits:

> — When Fang wants a hot meal he knows where he can go.
> — Fang has scads of socks—six pairs that match and twenty-seven singles
> (qtd. in Wilde, *Comedians* 209).

While the average '50s housewife was said to put in a 99.6-hour work week (Hymowitz 327), more time than her mother had spent, Diller's stage character never cleaned. According to Hymowitz, the ideal homemaker "sewed curtains, upholstered furniture, laid carpets, wallpapered bedrooms . . . took up bread making and home canning" (327). The home of Diller's stage persona, on the other hand, was a safety hazard. In this fantasy, her kitchen visitor experiences near death:

> Boy, do I have a greasy sink. I have watched bugs slide to their death. When the Food and Drug people arrived…. I was cooking. I was making a pudding and I knew something was wrong. I couldn't get the spoon out. They tried to stir it and the whole room went around…and then they wanted to take it to their lab to test it. Well, they had to. One of their guys was now stuck in it. So they took it to the lab. Are you ready? My pudding is bullet proof (*Are You Ready For Phyllis Diller?*).

As protagonist in this domestic world, she destroyed the order laid out for women. The routine continues:

> Supposing you are a housewife and you have goofed. Let's put it this way. It's 4:30 and you're still in bed. You know, that's getting pretty close to ogre time. When the beast comes home, the beauty better be ready. So here's the way you play that. You put a little eau cedar wax behind each ear. It makes you SMELL tired (*What's Left of Phyllis Diller?*).

As a housewife, Diller reverses the role of wife as subservient to her husband. In this routine, she tries to trick her husband into eating a dinner she has warmed in the clothes dryer. Since the oven had broken down, she made the best recovery she could:

> So I realized I would have to treat him rather graciously... So I read a couple of chapters of *Peyton Place* and a little Norman Vincent Peale. I even put on a dress (Ha, ha, ha), over my blue jeans. And when I say I kissed him, he thought he was in the wrong house, until one of the kids bit him. So I sat him down, I put this food in front of him, and right away he says, "You know I hate coconut." I said, "That's not coconut. It's lint" (*Phyllis Diller Laughs*).

Diller on the Dominance of Men

As the preceding routine suggests, the era of *Make Room for Daddy* and *Father Knows Best* did not invite direct attacks upon the dominant position of men in the society. When men were the targets, Diller's "put down" humor had to be carefully modulated. In the following routine she first makes fun of her own incompetence, but then she makes fun of her husband's expectations that she conform to his visions of housewife:

> He said, "I want you to be a little old-fashioned housewife. We'll start out by you dressing a chicken for Sunday dinner." He's got to be kidding. It took me three weeks to make the blouse. What's more, "I want you to dress old-fashioned. I want you to wear those little chintzy aprons." He should have told me you're supposed to wear something under them. You think you've seen a frightened Fuller Brush man? (*Phyllis Diller Laughs*).

This is one of the strongest examples of an attack on the cultural ideal of the homemaker. Diller follows it with an attack on the macho image held up as an ideal for men. Given the taboo nature of such an attack, she first paints a picture of herself as athletically incompetent.

> I was at the pool doing the Australian crawl, and my husband comes over to me and says, "You idiot, get in the pool." I can't do it in the pool! And he knows it. He's still coming on like James Cagney. It's been years now I've been analyzing it.... Men try forever to preserve the old football image. You know, it's so ridiculous with him. He's shaped like one. I lace him up every morning. He's still talking about his injuries. He was hurt once. In a huddle. Another time when the bench fell over backwards (*Phyllis Diller Laughs*).

The appeal of this subject matter to the common person helped sustain Diller's enormous popularity. Nevertheless, stage character and content alone do not create comedy; technique and pace are needed to bring on the laughter.

DILLER'S TECHNIQUE

Phyllis Diller sustained her success, not only by creating her self-mocking persona, but by mastering the craft of the joke itself. As the basis of her act, the line joke was chosen for its economy, word weight, and degree of truth (Wilde, *Comedians* 217-21). In delivery she mastered the timing of the set up, pause, and punch line (Wilde, *Writers* 272-3). She sought material that would have broad appeal:

> I work right in the center—food, sex, clothing, everyday things—I never predicate a gag on the audience having read something or having had to see a movie.... So, there's the rule: If every person in the audience doesn't get it at the same moment, I don't want it.... I only want boff, boff, boff, boff! I don't want giggles (qtd. in Wilde, *Comedians* 221).

As Diller says of her work, "It's a thousand one-liners" (qtd. in Wilde, *Comedians* 220).

> — I'm a back seat driver, I don't tell people how to drive, I have long arms (208).
> — I had to give up exercising—I can't stand the noise (209).

In each of these jokes the straight line comes first, then the pause, then the laugh line, with the laugh word(s) at the end of the joke. By using a "layering" form, she was able to build one joke upon another. She was told that Bob Hope's writers clocked her work and counted twelve jokes a minute, whereas Hope only averaged six jokes a minute. In her interview with Larry Wilde, she explains this technique:

> I'd lay something out and then top it . . . because silence makes me so nervous. You wouldn't believe it. Therefore, I always have these little phrases—one word, three words, four words—that at the end of each line is a laugh. Now, I'm building to a big punch or maybe I've given 'em a big punch, and I add, add, add, add, topper, topper, topper, topper, topper. . . that's one of my biggest things. It makes me different (qtd. in Wilde, *Comedians* 217).

Continuing the build with the layering technique allows Diller to stay with one subject, extending the wacky world of her persona. Even though each routine is made up of a series of one-liners, Diller covers only a few subjects in a performance, unlike, for example, Henny Youngman, who tells one unrelated joke after another (Allen 319). In this routine, Diller ridicules herself but, by extension, she ridicules the social pressure on housewives to make the feasts of

Thanksgiving and Christmas so special. Analysis, line by line, reveals that this is a series of one-liners about one subject.

> I was having my own troubles with that turkey. I learned the true meaning of the word, "fowl." Here's what I did.... I hung the body out the window. It was cold, I shut the window on the head, left the body outside, and I went on with my work. Everything was going great until I got this call from the ugly woman downstairs. "Phyllis, what is this stuff coming down the side of the building?" I wondered where it was going. Nobody told me to sew up the other end. . . .I said, "You wanna know what it is? Taste it." She did. They had to take her away. I wish they hadn't taken her through the lobby. Screaming for cranberries (*Are You Ready For Phyllis Diller?*).

Technically, the routine could be stopped at several points, and a switch made to another subject, but as long as the audience is responsive, Diller keeps building with them. She claims that many routines were built spontaneously through this interaction. Her Sukiyaki routine was developed at The Purple Onion the night that she had eaten in a sukiyaki restaurant. Sitting on the floor, getting her hand stepped on, trying to get up, all went into her routine which was built with the audience the very night of the dinner (*Standing Up for Women*).

Diller also occasionally improvised whole acts, as she did in her Sukiyaki routine: "If you're on and you're terribly creative, your channel is open. I went to my first sukiyaki dinner place ... and on the floor that night a great big bit grew." (qtd. in Wilde, *Comedians* 218). However, she is a traditional stand-up in that she never deviated from the use of the formal one-line joke as the basis of her routine. Her economy and sharp observation created an extremely high standard, which went far beyond the mechanical.

As a joke writer, Phyllis Diller was particularly attuned to the sound of words. In one-liners, the arrangement of the words gets the laugh. "They can't meander. The funny word must be at the end of the sentence" (220).

> — My mother told me how to cure Fang's hiccoughs.
> "Hold his head under water."
> — Fang loves crowds. He's not gregarious. He's a pick-pocket (208).

To Wilde, Diller tells the story of another writer who heard her routine on her mother-in-law, Moby Dick, in which she described the woman as "jello with a belt." The writer asked why Diller didn't describe her as "jello with hair." Diller answered that hair is a soft sound and would not have the weight of the consonant to bring the laugh. "Belt" is a "pow" word (220). You can hear this sensitivity toward the sound value of words in all her jokes: "Fang's got his father's tooth and his mother's lip" (208). The placement of "lip" at the end of the sentence ends the joke on a "pow" word. In the following joke the word arrangement as well as the sound weight result in laughter: "If I were a building I'd be condemned" (208).

In the '60s Diller read every joke that was sent to her and bought the ones that she wanted (219). Later in her career, she hired editors to read (219). Her top writer in the '60s, Mary McBride, a housewife with five children, lived in Janesville, Wisconsin. However, Diller generated most of her material herself (219). "Ideas come from life," Diller said in her interview on the *Standing Up for Women* panel. She spoke of how she would observe the airplane, make a joke about the door to the cockpit costing $50,000, replacing it with a beaded door, write it down, drop it in her purse and look at it later. Diller claimed that sensitivity to life and observation make a writer (*Standing Up for Women*). For Diller, the joke that will get the biggest laugh is the one that's based on the closest truth (216). Mel Brooks remarks on this phenomenon: "I found playing off truth got the best results. Observe and slightly exaggerate, and you have comedy" (qtd. in Wilde, *Writers* 5).

Diller gives this as an example of a joke based on close observation:

> There's one thing about this business that really frightens me, the bright lights—because when I was a housewife, if I ever had this much light on me, when I woke up, I had another kid (qtd. in Wilde, *Comedians* 216).

In one of her routines, she takes a swipe at the new wave of psychology, suggesting that it is easy now to avoid responsibility for behavior because one can blame one's parents. This one-liner looks at the psychology trend, but is ultimately based on careful observation of the terror a three year old can feel at being lost: "Do you know what happened to me? When I was three my parents sent me to the store for bubble gum. While I was gone, they moved" (*Phyllis Diller Laughs*).

Mort Sullivan, one of Bob Hope's writers, talked about the strange alchemy of writing comedy: "You can't teach intelligence or imagination, or how to observe life from a funny point of view. You can't teach somebody to be a mad, inspired genius like Mel Brooks. But given some of these qualities, you can probably teach them something about the mechanics" (qtd. in Wilde, *Writers* 272).

Phyllis Diller's technique helped her realize her comic genius. Through careful mastery of her delivery in timing and word arrangement, she magnetized her audience to her words. (In a live performance I saw in 1996, Diller told 15 jokes in 65 seconds.) By putting her finger on the cultural pulse, she was able to create a character who stood back and said sarcastically, "You've got to be kidding!" about the state of women's lives. Her jokes were based on observation from her own life, on her own experience as a woman, wife, and mother, and they politely disrupted the orderly monolith that had been given women as their world. By the end of the '60s and in the early '70s, that staid world had been shaken by the civil rights demonstrations, the peace movement, and the women's movement.

A younger comedian, Lily Tomlin, used the force of these social and political disruptions to swerve comedy off its traditional track.

Diller's comedy addressed groups of women who could laugh at their submission to unrealistic expectations. This was a welcome relief for women accustomed to the isolation of their own homes with little opportunity for group consciousness. Diller fomented no revolutions, but she helped make society aware of cultural excesses that limited women. By making fun of husbands, Diller was able to reverse the dominant joke content, which often made fun of wives. By presenting herself as an outrageously failed woman, her negative exemplar was able to tap into the subtle discontent in her audience. In her role as licensed spokesperson, she exposed the boundaries to personal growth erected by rigid and idealized standards for women.

In the history of women and stand-up comedy, Diller holds a unique place as the only mainstream professional female stand-up from 1955 to 1965, and one of a few (with Joan Rivers and Totie Fields) from 1965 to 1975. Even though all three used self-deprecating humor to win their following, all three shaped successful and courageous careers in the brutally competitive field of stand-up. Diller relentlessly pursued her career: "I know what I'm capable of and not to do it... would be a drag" (qtd. in Collier 6). By the sheer genius of her verbal and performance skill, Diller was able to create routines that kept hitting America's funny bone. Her consummate skill at crafting the joke made her not only a bankable star, but one of the first and most important women comedians.

As the stand-up stage expanded to include more women, such as Lily Tomlin and Roseanne, Diller stood as a forerunner. She did what no woman had done before or since; she broke the gender barrier in stand-up. Diller was the test case that proved that a woman comedian could be as good as, even better than, most men in what Elayne Boosler calls the "blood sport" of comedy (qtd. in Barreca, *Penguin* 74)[1]. To assail her because, by today's standards, she isn't "enough" is to unjustly minimize her significance. Just as James Meredith had to take a lonely walk up to Ole Miss to break the race barrier, so Diller had to take that first step onto the male-dominated stage of stand-up to break the gender barrier. That she was received with laughter begins the tale that includes many women, beneficiaries of Diller's trailblazing efforts.

Chapter Three
Lily Tomlin
Breaking with Tradition

> ERNESTINE
> One, ringy-dingy, two, ringy-dingy. A gracious good afternoon. This is Miss Tomlin at the telephone company. Have I reached the party to whom I am speaking? Mr. Veedle, you owe us a balance of $23.64; when may we expect payment? P...pardon? When what freezes over? No. No. Mr. Veedle, Mr. Veedle, you are not dealing with just anyone's fool. I am a high school grad-u-ate. Now then, when may we expect payment? Oh, Mr. Veedle, I don't see why you're kicking up such a ruckus, when according to our files, your present bank balance, plus stocks, securities and other holdings amount to exactly thirt... p..pardon? Privileged information? (*Ernestine: Peak Experiences*).

AFTER THREATENING MR. VEEDLE WITH THE END OF HIS PHONE SERVICE and a visit from a burly phone repairman, Ernestine then plays Mr. Veedle a recording of his own voice during some shady dealing. At this point, Mr. Veedle capitulates and Ernestine ends the conversation: "And Mr. Veedle, there's no reason on earth for you to feel personally persecuted. We may be the only phone company in town, but we screw everybody!" *(Ernestine: Peak Experiences)*.

    Tomlin's satire signaled a change for women and comedy. As her characterization of Ernestine shows, Tomlin had no compunction in ridiculing any institutionalized authority, even the multi-conglomerate phone company. This confident comedy departs significantly from earlier women's comedy, which by necessity made accommodations to the culture. Bold, bright, and blasting of social injustice, Tomlin directs her comedy as a weapon of change. As a forceful demonstration of the expanding roles for women, Tomlin breaks with women's comedy of earlier decades, which restricted female comedians to stereotypical roles. Unlike the work of Phyllis Diller, the comedy of Lily Tomlin requires little decoding, primarily because she is not obliged to live in two worlds, one traditional and one modern. Tomlin's comedy starts from the premise that women are free to use their intelligence, their perceptions, and their experience to create a vital performance art, which will contribute a unique and important viewpoint. In this way, Tomlin and her primary writer and partner, Jane Wagner, become spokespersons and models for a comedy of satiric substance.

BIOGRAPHY

Born to working class parents on September 1, 1939, the older of two children, Lily Tomlin creates comedy that reflects her understanding of common people. Her father, who worked as a toolmaker for The Commonwealth Brass Co. of Detroit, encouraged her comedy, and she was particularly close to him. In their apartment, where her mother was a housewife, Lily and her brother did comedy routines based on their relatives (originally from the farm country of Kentucky and Tennessee) and neighbors in their predominately white working class neighborhood. Tomlin made her theatrical debut at Wayne State University in *The Madwoman of Chaillot* when she stole the show by extending her walk-on part with a comic improvisation. Leaving Wayne State after two years to try and make it in New York, she found the place inhospitable and returned quickly to Detroit to work in coffee houses where she introduced some of her characters, such as The Tasteful Lady.

When she returned to New York in 1965, Tomlin worked in improvisation clubs such as The Improv and Cafe Au Go Go, again doing her characters. In 1966 Tomlin appeared on *The Gary Moore Show* and *The Merv Griffin Show*. In March 1968, Vincent Canby of the *New York Times* predicted her success when he saw her in Rod Warren's comedy revue, *Photo Finish*. In 1969 George Schlatter, executive producer of the comedy variety show *Rowan and Martin's Laugh-In*, offered Tomlin a contract. Tomlin remained with *Laugh-In* through 1973 and on the show debuted many of her famous characters: Ernestine, the high strung Suzie Sorority, and her precocious five year old, Edith Ann. The most important comedy variety show of its day, *Laugh-In* encouraged Tomlin's taste for the off-beat, the misfit, and the satirical in her character portraits.

During this early phase, Tomlin also performed in nightclubs and produced three albums, *This Is a Recording* (1971) featuring Ernestine, *And That's the Truth* (1972) featuring Edith Ann, and *Modern Scream*. The Ernestine album, released by Polydor, won a Grammy award from the National Academy of Recording Arts and Sciences for the year's best comedy recording. In this period Tomlin also made television appearances on *The Flip Wilson Show*, doing pieces as Edith Ann and Ernestine and comic sketches with Flip Wilson and his guest artists. When *Laugh-In* went off the air in 1973, Tomlin turned to television specials, Broadway, and film.

In 1971 Tomlin met Jane Wagner, and the two have been together ever since as partners and professional collaborators. Wagner's impact on Tomlin's work has been profound as even an incomplete record of their combined projects reveals. Originally Tomlin hired Wagner to write for her Edith Ann character. When Tomlin saw Wagner's television piece, *J.T.*, about a young boy in Harlem, Tomlin was so impressed with the humanity of the writing that she wrote Wagner and asked her to help give some of the same depth to her Edith Ann character. Wagner didn't answer for months, but when she finally sent material, Tomlin convinced her to come out to Pasadena to help her produce it. Although Wagner had won a Peabody for the writing of *J.T.*, she claims she would not have written comedy without the letter from Tomlin (Riley).

The success of their collaboration hinges on mutual respect. In an interview in 2003 with Janelle Riley from *Back Stage West*, Jane Wagner reported: "We can argue and still respect each other. Our styles are different in that I don't have the confidence Lily has. She's quick to commit to something where I'm always questioning." Tomlin responded, "Even if I disagree heartily about something, I believe Jane might know better than I do. Especially if it's about making something deeply dramatic and impactful work." Wagner commented that she admires Tomlin for her "fierceness," and Tomlin gave Wagner credit for common sense and depth of sensitivity. That sensitivity turns to the world about them as well as to work. Tomlin said of Wagner: "She can slice onions very thin and can teach any animal how to do something. She taught our goat to shake hands."

Wagner's name appears with Tomlin's as writer and creator on the Edith Ann album, *And That's the Truth* (1972). The 1973 television shows *Lily* and *The Lily Tomlin Show* were written by Tomlin, Wagner, Richard Pryor, and others. In 1975 the pair produced and wrote the album *Modern Scream* featuring Tomlin in a number of character sketches, including Suzie Sorority, Judith Beasley, and Sister Boogie Woman. In her acceptance speech at the 1977 Tony Awards for the Broadway show *Appearing Nitely!* Tomlin gave the following tribute to Jane Wagner: "One very special person is Jane Wagner whose brilliant talent has contributed more to what I have done than any other person I know, and with whom I share this honor totally" *(Appearing Nitely!)*. In 1981, the Emmy Award-winning television special *Lily Sold Out!* was executively produced by Tomlin and Wagner, and partially written by Wagner. One of the highlights of their careers has been the play *The Search for Signs of Intelligent Life in the Universe* (1986), written by Jane Wagner as a one-woman show for Tomlin.

The one-hour television special and the one-woman show forms gave Tomlin more concentrated exposure for her popular characters. On March 16, 1973, CBS presented a one-hour comedy special, *The Lily Tomlin Show*. Written by nine writers, Tomlin was featured in extended skits of many of her existing characters: Ernestine, Edith Ann, Mrs. Beasley, and The Tasteful Lady. *The Lily Tomlin Show* demonstrates Tomlin's bent for political satire, as Nixon speaks to Ernestine, threatening violence toward Ralph Nader. *Lily*, Tomlin's second television special, shown on CBS on November 2, 1973, received an Emmy for Best Variety Music or Comedy Special. Her many albums offered fans in-depth skits with Ernestine, Edith Ann, and a combination of other early characters.

The work of Tomlin/Wagner reveals a turn towards a more defined comic aesthetic, manifest in their first Broadway one-woman show, *Lily Tomlin Appearing Nitely!* (1977). Co-written and co-produced with Wagner, the show won Tomlin a special Tony. From this point forward in her career, the performer's stage and television work gives credit to Wagner as writer, co-creator, or co-producer. There is a movement from shorter sketch pieces to longer sketches with more developed characters and towards deeper comic exploration of serious themes. For example, in *Appearing Nitely!* Glenna analyzes the '60s and Crystal reflects on her life as a quadriplegic. Following in the footsteps of one of her models, the stage actress Ruth Draper, Tomlin proves herself a solo actress popular enough to fill a Broadway house for several months.

Another milestone in defining their new artistic identity can be seen in the originality of the Emmy award winning show *Lily Sold Out!* (1981), which reveals structural and thematic advances over the more derivative television special *The Lily Tomlin Show* (1973). While *The Lily Tomlin Show* is based on the television specials of its time, interweaving random monologues and songs with the comic sketches of guest artists (including Richard Pryor), the later television special *Lily Sold Out!* is an entirely integrated piece with one theme. As the featured performer in a series of short sketches, Tomlin ridicules the entertainment industry. By asserting values in opposition to the entertainment industry, Tomlin/Wagner announce their commitment to a new comedy, one that avoids glitz and affirms art, a type that will mark future work of Tomlin/Wagner as they progress.

In 1986 Tomlin was awarded the Tony for Best Actress in a leading role in a play for her performance in Wagner's one-woman show *The Search for Signs of Intelligent Life in the Universe*. The play represents a unique stage in their collaboration because, unlike previous work, credit for the writing goes entirely to Wagner. Even if Tomlin underrates her own writing, ("In the beginning I was forced to make up stuff, but it was mediocre") it is indisputable that the force of their combined creativity has resulted in a vital collection of sustained characters (qtd. in Lavin E2). The revival of the show, beginning on Broadway in 2000, was also produced to wide acclaim.

Wagner's play and Tomlin's performance stand as a monument to a focused and unbroken career line guided by clear artistic and political beliefs. Unapologetically feminist in tone, far reaching in theme, the play is a genuine search by its sixteen characters, all played by Tomlin, for meaning in a fractured universe. In 1992, the play was made into an HBO movie, and is now available in video stores. For the film, Tomlin won several awards including Funniest Actress in a Motion Picture by the American Comedy Awards of 1992. The partnership of Tomlin and Wagner spanned the century, when Tomlin began performing *Search* again in 2000. After a Broadway run, under Wagner's direction, Tomlin played it in several cities including L.A. and Seattle. Of the 2000 New York production a *Variety* reviewer commented: "There's something magical about a show that can bring you to tears of laughter and sympathy at virtually the same time." By 2003, however, the L.A. production of the show was taking a toll on Tomlin, then sixty-three, who reportedly had to stop occasionally to take sips from a glass of water (Kendt 11).

Tomlin has had a rich and varied career as a television and film actress. From 1996 to 1998 Tomlin played Murphy's boss in the sitcom *Murphy Brown*. In 2002 she joined Martin Sheen and the award-winning cast of NBC's *The West Wing* to play the president's secretary, Debbie Fiderer. For her screen debut she played Linnea, a gospel singer and mother of two deaf children, in the 1975 film *Nashville*. For her role, Tomlin won an Oscar nomination and Best Supporting Actress by the New York Film Critics Circle. Jane Fonda and Dolly Parton joined Tomlin in the film *9 to 5* (1980). In *Big Business* (1988) Tomlin joined forces with Bette Midler.

Tomlin played Miss Jane Hathaway in the film version of *The Beverly Hillbillies* (1993). Her acting in *Short Cuts* (1994) earned her an American Comedy Award as Funniest Supporting Actress. The HBO film *The Celluloid Closet* (1996), which Tomlin produced and narrated, was nominated for an Emmy. *The Incredible Shrinking Woman* (1981), which Jane Wagner wrote, merited a Best Actress award from the Fantafestival. Other films include *The Late Show* (1977) and *All of Me* (1984), Carl Reiner's comic film about a rich woman who takes over the body of a man, played by Steve Martin. *Flirting with Disaster* (1996), *Krippendorf's Tribe* (1998), *Tea with Mussolini* (1999), *Disney's the Kid* (2000), and *Orange County* (2002) are a few of her many other films.

In 2003 Tomlin was awarded the distinguished "Kennedy Center Mark Twain Prize for American Humor." Only five other recipients have received this esteemed honor, given in honor of Mark Twain who was "a fearless observer of society, who startled many while delighting many more with his uncompromising perspective of social injustice and personal folly." Tomlin's award reads in part:

> Her comedy is meaningful because, like Twain's, it expresses truths we already recognize unconsciously, and it allows us to embrace our frailties without shame or embarrassment. As Twain before her and Jane Austin before him, Lily Tomlin's communion with her characters creates an undeniable intimacy with her audiences, giving everyone a feeling of connectedness in the process.

Tomlin responded to the honor by saying she was humbled to be in the company of past recipients: Richard Pryor, Jonathan Winters, Carl Reiner, Whoopi Goldberg, and Bob Newhart, and she saluted Twain since "he imparted a strong and vital social consciousness that still resonates today" (Tomlin's website). This award further legitimizes Tomlin's rank as a comedian who serves as a licensed spokesperson for society, using the path of laughter to point out its missteps.

THE EFFECT OF THE WOMEN'S MOVEMENT ON THE WORK OF TOMLIN/WAGNER

The contrast between Diller's careful resistance of the patriarchy and the Tomlin/Wagner bold rejection of it can be partially understood in light of the momentum of the women's movement. The 1970s highlighted inequities between men's lives and women's lives and called for, in Gloria Steinem's words, "a transformation of the patriarchy, not just integration into it by a few women" (9). Lily Tomlin was a political activist in this decade, not just in her feminist comedy, but in her support of women candidates like Bella Abzug and in her support of groups like Women Against Violence Against Women, who were trying to improve women's lives and status (Levine 231, 210).

In the fields of art, sport, politics, law, science, education, and work women were making strides and assuming positions of power and authority as never before. Where this power and authority were denied them, women used demonstrations, boycotts, and pickets to foreground their causes and insist on change. The decade opened with the largest demonstration by women up to that time, when 50,000 women marched down Fifth Avenue to celebrate the fiftieth anniversary of women's suffrage (Levine 29). In 1972, Shirley Chisholm, a black woman, unsuccessfully ran for president. In 1974, Ella Grasso of Connecticut became the first woman to be elected governor in her own right (12,14). In 1971, Billie Jean King became the highest paid tennis player of all men and women in that year (8).

In 1973, the Supreme Court legalized abortion in its *Roe v. Wade* decision, following successful arguments by two women lawyers (12). Massachusetts, in 1974, elected Elaine Noble to the state legislature, the first self-declared lesbian to be elected to state office (14). Though not recognized by the hierarchy in 1974, eleven women were ordained Episcopal priests; in 1976 the hierarchy reversed its stand and ordained the first woman and recognized the unofficial ordination (14). Women won equal right to credit with the Opportunity Act. Sarah Caldwell became the director of the Opera Company of Boston (42), and in 1976 she conducted Beverly Sills at the Metropolitan Opera, thus becoming the first woman to conduct the Metropolitan Opera (42). *Time* magazine joined the decade's recognition of women when it honored ten women on its cover, replacing its usual "Man of the Year." In 1978 more women than men entered American colleges for the first time in history (22).

In this *zeitgeist*, Tomlin and Wagner led a current in women's comedy performance that took its force from the heady days of the women's movement. Stressing feminist views by rejecting the status quo for women and suggesting change, their characters urge a reassessment of conventional roles for women. As lesbians appealing to a mainstream audience, their work did not proclaim their sexual preference, but it did present alternatives to the mainstream culture that typically identified all women as heterosexual, wives, and mothers. Many of their characters, like Crystal and Sister Boogie Woman, identify themselves as single and independent women.

SHIFTING THE PARADIGM: TOMLIN'S ROLE OF COMEDIAN AS SHAMAN

Although Mintz's paradigm of stand-up as negative exemplar and licensed spokesperson applies easily to traditional women stand-ups such as Phyllis Diller, it is a less successful frame when the form of comedy expands and the hegemonic culture is disrupted. Two shifts that repositioned Tomlin's work in relationship to the traditional comic persona of negative exemplar were her commitment to character comedy and her feminism. While the loser persona of the traditional negative exemplar has the advantage for the comedian of uniting the audience both in ridicule of and empathy for "the loser," the loser persona conflicts with the positive image of women asserted by feminism. In addition, as the forms of comedy expanded with the work of the "New Wave" comedians like Nichols and May and Lenny Bruce, the negative exemplar persona was no longer the only option for a comedian. Rather than a negative exemplar, Tomlin chose a different comic persona to ground her social values and to serve as a springboard for her multiple characters.

Discerning the parallels between Tomlin's work and shamanism highlights the contrast between Tomlin's comedy and that of her traditional predecessors. By replacing the traditional comedian's role as negative exemplar with a broader role of comedian as visionary, Tomlin's comedy is similar to the healing work of the shaman. Anthropologist E. T. Kirby's definition of shamanism "as the practice of trance for the purpose of curing the sick" (6), applies to two aspects of Tomlin's work. First, Tomlin uses a transformational acting technique related to the shaman's "possession," and second, Tomlin's satire works toward a "cure" for society.

First, "comedic possession," a process whereby "another soul takes possession of her body" (qtd. in Stone 15) is a term used by Tomlin's partner, Jane Wagner, to describe Tomlin's method of absolute immersion into her characters. Although all actors transform through concentration into their characters, the degree to which Tomlin "disappears" into her characters is unique. The intensity of Tomlin's transformations that I observed in a live performance of *Search* reminded me of a transformation I observed of a medicine man in a Navajo Blessingway ceremony outside Tuba City, Arizona. In that ceremony, the medicine man, an uncle of the Navajo teenager who was the subject of the ceremony, was an ordinary man outside the sacred place. Once the medicine man entered the sacred place, he visibly transformed into another person, appearing taller and more powerful and influencing me into another plane of consciousness. In a similar manner, Tomlin's "comedic possession" breaks into another reality. Her reality, like that described by Kirby of shamanistic illusion, "break[s] the surface of reality... to cause the appearance of a super-reality that is 'more real' than the ordinary" (14). I participated with Tomlin as she created a "super reality," which invited me into her theatrical ritual, one that ultimately pointed toward social cure.

Second, the spirit behind the Tomlin/Wagner satire, visionary, truth telling, and healing, points to a better way for society, a curative path. As she expressed in the following interview, Tomlin views her comedy as healing: "When it's over, you're better for it. You come away with something" (qtd. in Robinson 187). More specifically, the Tomlin/Wagner characters suggest another direction for society than the hierarchical one which has cast aside so many people. As Marilyn French observed, "Underlying the gentle laughter that is a Tomlin/Wagner hallmark is the conviction that we have some power to alter the course of our world as well as our own lives" (34).

The strategies of the shamanistic comedian create a different comic dynamic than those of the negative exemplar comedian. Whereas Diller's negative persona harshly ridicules both herself and Fang, Tomlin uses a more humanistic approach to her characters. In her characters, she exposes vulnerabilities that her audience can relate to, and through laughter strives toward a "cure." Tomlin works to bring her characters "up a peg," as Elizabeth Stone suggests, "in revealing the humanness of those in whom it had not been so apparent" (15). These strategies play out in characters such as Mrs. Judith Beasley and Suzie Sorority—women who do not think independently. Because they adhere too strictly to rigid gender roles that distort their personalities, limit their possibilities, and give their power away to those who would continue to subjugate women, the behavior of these characters is often in conflict with Tomlin's beliefs. Yet Tomlin brings out their humanity as they discover the depth of their disappointment in false dreams.

In this sketch from the 1973 award winning television special, *The Lily Tomlin Show*, Mrs. Beasley makes a shattering discovery. Playing "an ordinary woman" in a TV commercial for a laundry soap named "GRRR!," Judith begins by endorsing the product. She begins with a controlled robotic voice, but as reality seeps in, she becomes frenzied:

> "GRRR!" contains a new additive called "carnivore" which seeks out and gobbles up stains like a thousand tiny little piranha fish. To prove it, I have brought some samples from my own family wash.... Look at these grass stains on Billy's chinos; these are really tough; and here these lipstick stains on my husband's collar. Well, anyway, I am only going to take, um. I am only going to take half a cup of uh, GRRR! You only need half a cup because it's concentrated. See, you can actually feel it coming on for weeks and weeks. He's been so indifferent no matter how hard I tried to please him. Because it's concentrated you save money because you use less and less, and less time at

> home, all those nights he said he was going bowling. I have just been kidding myself like some kind of fool. [Angry] Well, the hell with you.... [shouting into mouth of washing machine] Well, you want to know something? Billy isn't yours!

Judith has bought too willingly into the romantic myth of marital bliss, but rather than criticize, Tomlin humanizes the character by exposing the depth of her pain. Her betrayal is heightened by Tomlin's initial presentation of Judith's character as tidy in appearance, making a credible spokesperson for the white, middle-class American, happy homemaker from Calumet City, Illinois. Stiff and robotic, Judith says her lines as if memorized:

> Hi, I am not a professional actress. I am a real person. I am not here to sell you a product but to give you some good consumer advice. I was an impulse shopper of the worst kind. I would buy anything on the shelf at eye level. I would even buy day old and fresh bread the same day.... I was just not using good sense. Like the time I bought a box of Pampers. Our son Billy was six years old and had been house broke more than a year. When my husband questioned me I had to think quickly. I said I was pregnant. Luckily, it slipped his mind and never came up again.... Remember, impulse buying is a bad habit. It can break you, if you don't break it (*Modern Scream*).

By portraying sympathetic characters that have been duped by gender expectations, Tomlin shifts the satire to the cultural values of the patriarchy and away from the person. Another character, Suzie Sorority, represents everything the white, heterosexual American girl ought to be: bright, perky, and dependent upon all the props of the patriarchy. Even more than Judith Beasley, Suzie is lost because she does not realize that the social system she endorses will drain her of intelligence, passion, and individuality. Portrayed on the album cover of *Modern Scream* with shoulder length blond hair turned up neatly at the ends, Suzie's favorite expression is: "I thought I was going to barf." In this excerpt from a sorority meeting, Suzie passionately expresses her views on the future direction of sorority life. With breathlessness and a slight lisp, she talks at the speed of light:

> Madame Chairperson, may I address the half session? Now I may be only Song Leader of the sorority, but on the motion on the floor about wearing white dresses to the second rush party, now just a second you guys, now we voted to wear white dresses and white heels, and now Sybil over there is complaining that we look like nurses. Well, by golly, I say we ought to have the gumption to look like nurses. . . Blackball this Buffy Woodstock. The fact that she refused to wear hose to the preference party, when we the hostesses had to brave this heat in hose, is proof to me of pure down right rad lib orneriness. Just a second. On the tour of the rooms she saw my bulletin board with

a picture of the Lennon Sisters she said, as if to herself, "Wow, I don't believe it!" And inside myself, I asked myself, "Do I want her for a sister? No!" (*Modern Scream*).

Because she is such an exaggeration of type, Suzie is more an object of ridicule than Judith Beasley, but her vitality is attractive and somewhat humanizing. More than Suzie's character, Tomlin ridicules a culture that encourages young women to be vacuous.

Of all Tomlin's characters, Ernestine is one of the most complex because while she is an arm of corporate America, she also enjoys her own sensuality and her use of power for kind purposes. "When it comes to power, I am like a moth to flame," Ernestine said as she sat in red shorts, legs crossed, for an interview with Joan Rivers on *The Johnny Carson Show (Ernestine: Peak Experiences)*. Even when she is most rigid, a fingertip will disappear down the front of her blouse. This particular combination of the politically barbed and the sensually charged is pure Tomlin, but it serves to keep Ernestine human and multi-dimensional. Ernestine's physical presentation belies her ruthlessness. Her large black and white earrings highlight sparkling eyes, intent on mischief. Her mouth, painted like a red bow, houses a little darting tongue which both wets her lips and punctuates her pronouncements. Her flared skirt reveals long legs, usually crossed at the knee with the calves pressed tightly against each other. Her black shoes, with their ankle straps and open toe, accentuate Ernestine's shapely calves. She occasionally exposes a human side as in this conversation with a wife who is worried because her husband's phone has been busy for more than an hour and a half. The operator listens in on the conversation and reports back to the wife:

> Just a minute, let me listen now. Mr. Norman and some woman are talking about your son in Korea. Excuse me, but Mrs. Norman, "Bok Choy" seems a strange name for a boy from Pleasantville. You say you don't have a son in Korea? That's odd; Mr. Norman does. Oh, Mrs. Norman, I am so sorry. I am so sorry that you had to learn it this way. But we at the phone company do like to keep families in touch. No, Mrs. Norman, listen to Ernestine, turn off the gas! I'll plug you into his line and you can hear every word the bastard's saying... (*This is a Recording*).

As Tomlin and Wagner's work grew, they concentrated less on characters who have been misled by the patriarchy and more on characters who have been brutally treated by it, the misfit and outcast. By virtue of their independence from an oppressive system and their positive personal spirit, these characters offer an alternative to the exclusivity and deprivation of the hegemony. In this sense, Tomlin inhabits her role of comedian as licensed spokesperson by embracing those different from the mainstream. Tomlin's admiration of the improvisational character actress, Elaine May, affected her comedic direction as she developed her role as licensed spokesperson.

LILY TOMLIN AND JANE WAGNER AS LICENSED SPOKESPERSONS

Tomlin saw in the improvisational comedy of Mike Nichols and Elaine May how, as Tom Brokow commented, "comedy could act as a catalyst in a nation's reassessment of its own myths" (*The Best of Nichols and May*). Acting in the 1950s when the nation raised conventionality to religious stature, Nichols and May's comedy undermined convention and provoked thought. Stretching the boundary of acceptable topics for comedy to include sex, adultery, motherhood, patriotism, advertising, and television itself, their brilliantly improvised character comedy set a standard for a generation of comics to come. As one of the few women comics in the succeeding generation, Tomlin developed from their model. Tomlin and her brother, Richard, played the Nichols and May album *Improvisations to Music* every day for two years (*Who Makes You Laugh?*). With a comic tone similar to Nichols and May's, Tomlin's spirited and satiric comedy addressed sociopolitical issues of her day.

Tomlin has paid tribute to Elaine May as her inspiration: "There was nothing like Elaine May with her voice, her timing and her attitude" (*Who Makes You Laugh?*). Traces of her most popular character, Ernestine, can be seen in May's earlier portrayal of a phone operator. Ernestine's nasal twang, superiority, and unflappability come through in this Nichols and May sketch, "Telephone," in which a man (Nichols) calls information for a number and loses his last dime in the telephone. The indomitable operator (May) not only refuses to return the dime, but leaves the man servile and frustrated before her icy authority.

> OPERATOR
> Information is a free service, sir. When you hang up, your di-em will be returned to you.
> MAN
> Miss, I know it's in there . . . It's my last dime, I have no change, my car has broken down, and I'm an hour late for a very important appointment. So you can see that... Hello?
> OPERATOR
> Information.
> MAN
> Oh, no. Miss, please return my dime.
> OPERATOR
> Sir, I cannot return your di-em to you until you hang up. When you hang up, you di-em will be returned (*The Best of Mike Nichols and Elaine May*).

Remarkable similarities to May's operator can be seen in this excerpt of Ernestine from *This Is a Recording*, "Boswick 9." In this sketch Tomlin, like May, puts a customer on the defensive after the customer has claimed the loss of her dime.

> May I have the number from which you are dialing? Is that "b" as in "boy," Boswick, ni-en, ni-en, 6-5-0? May I safely assume that is a pay station? And may I have your name and address please? Thank you. M'am, we will send you your dime as soon as we have checked the validity of your claim.

Tomlin found in Nichols and May a satiric comedy of character with an inspiring level of risk-taking and intelligence. "This more cerebral material was important to me" *(Who Makes You Laugh?)*. Since Nichols and May did not work from a script, their act had a startling vitality. At the same time that Tomlin emulated the cultural insight for which Nichols and May had become known, her characterizations of Ernestine, Suzie Sorority, and Judith Beasley show that Tomlin was also influenced by the range of characters they portrayed. Nichols and May's comic strategies of characterization, word play, power play, role reversal, and psychological insight became strategies that Tomlin would employ in her own work.

One demonstration of Nichols and May's cultural insight was their consistent ability to place a comic crack in the '50s portrait of the perfect family. As such, the Nichols and May humor was a revolutionary explosion against well-behaved families and strict gender roles. The following excerpts from the Broadway show *An Evening with Nichols and May* (1960) demonstrate their commitment to truth in comedy. Delivering a more realistic family portrait than that which television offered, "Mother and Son" features a mother who reduces her rocket scientist son to babbling idiocy because he has not called her:

> MOTHER
> Arthur, I sat by that phone all day Friday. All night Friday night.
> SON
> I kept thinking, I gotta' call mom.
> MOTHER
> All day Sunday. Your father said to me, "Phyllis, eat something, you'll faint." I said, "No, Harold, no. I don't want my mouth to be full when my son calls me."
> SON
> Mother, I was sending up Vanguard. I didn't have a second.

Tomlin's work in collaboration with Wagner shows a growing realization of her ideal to create a comedy of genuine substance and cultural commentary. Their work, particularly *Appearing Nitely!* (1977), *Lily Sold Out* (1981), and *The*

Search For Signs of Intelligent Life in the Universe (1986), presents a comedy that expects the audience to respond not as passive absorbers of spectacle, but as thoughtful participants in their own culture. In exchange for the audience's intellectual engagement, Tomlin and Wagner genuinely entertain them with characters that are always more than they seem and whose position as misfits casts a fascinating light on what we consider normal. From outside the mainstream, these figures often see into the hypocrisy, greed, and intolerance that mark the dominant culture. Tomlin and Wagner develop a comedy that evokes both a compassion for their characters as well as an intelligent reassessment of the systems which pushed their characters to the edge. In some cases, as the physically disabled character, Crystal, points out, political activism is held as a logical next step.

A deepening commitment to their role as licensed spokespersons becomes clear in several of the characters from *Appearing Nitely!*. When Tomlin and Wagner present their first male character, Rick, the barfly, we see their feminism take a new twist, as the comic exaggeration of machismo reveals a sad and empty life, showing the suffocating effect of gender restrictions not only on women but on men. Chugging beers, Tomlin, as Rick, talks to his imaginary buddy about "getting lucky":

> See anything hot? Hey, check out the short skirt with the big head lamps. I wouldn't kick that out of bed.... She sticks out in all the right places, doesn't she? You want her? I'll get her for you, as a present. Hey, what's that you're drinking? Grasshopper? That's liable to put hair on your chest, Button Nose. Hey, I'm Rick.... I got a pal over here, he thinks you're a real looker. Yeah. I do too. He saw you first, so I promised him. He can have first crack at you. Hey, where are you goin'? Hey, Fortune, where are you goin? Hey, Fortune, come over here! Come over here! Hey, Fortune, come over here! (*Appearing Nitely!*).

Had the sketch ended here, Rick would remain a funny but brutal male stereotype; however, he returns to the bartender and shows him a photograph of a little boy, gradually revealing that both his wife and child have left him. "She was studying to improve her memory, forgot she had a husband.... You can't blame her, right? Smart guy, college educated, you can't blame her. I'd like to see my kid, though" (*Appearing Nitely!*). By exposing Rick's vulnerability, Tomlin and Wagner elicit compassion for him and invite audience reflection on repressive male gender role restrictions.

As the work of Tomlin/Wagner developed they created more characters that were misfits, but outcasts full of wisdom, a version of the comic archetype, the wise fool. Three examples of these characters, Tess, Crystal, and Sister Boogie Woman, come from Tomlin's 1977 Broadway show, *Appearing Nitely!*. Infectiously positive in spirit, their undefeated view of life works to confront the very stereotypes by which they are usually dismissed.

Tess, a bag lady, narrates the show and demonstrates the Tomlin/Wagner reach for characters on the margins of society. A video recording of the play, documenting a performance at the Huntington Hartford Theater in Los Angeles, shows a sudden burst of vitality in all her limbs when Tomlin's body transforms into Tess. Her knees bend, her arms surge upward and she takes space on the stage, waving to each section of the audience: "How ya do'in? How ya do'in? How ya do'in?" The actor's voice lowers in range, her eyes magnify, and she stares straight into the audience: "Did ya miss me? I just got out." Tess darts out toward the audience holding up something in one hand, "Ya wanna buy a potholder? I could use automatic mind command; I could make you buy one. How about you? I made them when I was inside to keep myself from going nuts" (*Appearing Nitely!*). With her energy and sense of fun, Tess charms the audience; she lures them into her view of reality by exposing her side of things: "[The doctors] don't like people who think they're God, because they think they're God." As guide, she establishes a safety zone where for a short time the world can be seen through her window.

Another of these marginalized characters is Crystal, a quadriplegic in a wheel chair. Crystal's portrait urges a more central role for disabled in society and encourages laws that evidence that respect. To introduce Crystal, Tomlin comes onto the stage and sets down a simple stool. Standing, she explains her equipment:

> This is a wheelchair. And this space-aged invention attached here has a mouth piece, and is nicknamed a joy stick. By blowing or puffing into it, the chair moves forward, by sucking or sipping it slams into reverse. Turning being a combination of sips and puffs. And this is a CD antenna. (singing) "Drifting along with the breeze . . .Pledging my love to the wind. . ." Hi! My name is Crystal, The Terrible Tumbleweed! My body is paralyzed, neck down, and I got a sunburn.

By asking the audience to visualize a woman in a wheelchair on the stage of a comedy show, Tomlin and Wagner demonstrate their intention to explore controversial subjects. In this portrait there is not one moment of self-pity; rather the audience meets a funny and thoughtful woman who is fed up with the condescension and ignorance society has toward her.

> **BYSTANDER**
> Oh, my God! How tragic! I cannot look, I just cannot look.
> **CRYSTAL**
> [normal, cheery voice]
> One year seven months now I'm on the road coast to coast, all by wheel chair. When I get to California I will go hang gliding off Big Sur. I will be the first quadriplegic to do so, possibly the last.

Once the audience becomes comfortable with Crystal, she confides in them the necessity of direct political action on behalf of the disabled.

> Each morning twelve million of us slam our big old bony asses into a wheelchair and sit. When I say, sit, baby, I mean sit. Might as well, once you get to where you're going, you can't get through the door, anyway, too narrow. I had a friend got caught in a revolving door. We had to buy the building. . . .
> BYSTANDER VOICE
> Boo! Hiss! Did she say sex? My God, why can't these people just leave well enough alone?
> CRYSTAL
> More or less what Davy's mother said, when she caught us together in his iron lung.

By daring to put an image of a physically disabled person on the stage, Tomlin/Wagner announce their belief in a comedy that deals in reality, that confronts pain, and that believes that society, if sensitized, will act compassionately toward those who are marginalized. Originally dropped from the HBO movie of the show, the portrait of Crystal was restored in the 1992 home video version, produced by Tomlin/Wagner.

Another marginalized group, the aged, is represented by Sister Boogie Woman, who embodies the spirit of vitality that symbolizes what is best in *Appearing Nitely!*. She not only contradicts negative stereotypes of the aged, but she also stands for an open embrace of life, a spirit of exuberance:

> I FEEL JOYFUL TONIGHT! I FEEL A DEEP DOWN JOY! . . . I tell you, I have received so many cards and letters recently. They all start off, "Sister Boogie Woman, I don't know how to tell you how my life has changed since I've added boogie to my heart." Now you might be asking yourselves, "What's that old seventy-seven-year-old woman talkin' about when she talks about all this boogie?" You say to me, "Just what, Sister Boogie Woman, is boogie? How do I know if I got it? If I don't got it, how can I get it?" Well, I'm gonna tell you, friends and neighbors. Boogie is when you're seventy-seven years old, you've got a pack on your back, and your teeth in a jar, and those teeth are smiling.... Boogie's not a meaning. Boogie's a feeling. Don't try to understand it. Try to feel it in your pleasure. BOOGIE IS FIRE IN YOUR LIFE!

By virtue of her enthusiasm, Sister Boogie Woman invites an audience to loosen its own grip on reality and look at life as full of possibility. Like Tess and Crystal, Sister Boogie Woman unfolds a vision where hope and joy are possible. By embodying her characters so fully, Tomlin invites the viewer to know another world. "Her gift is for…the meticulous detail with which she supplies her [characters]" pointed out Walter Kerr in reviewing the Broadway production (63). Even though Tess delivers the message from her space chums that "the world is cracked," she nonetheless manages a full life, as Tomlin suggests, a life worth caring about.

TECHNIQUE

Tomlin's comic form significantly contributes to her overall artistic effectiveness. By using a complete physicalization she invites each character to take over her voice and body. My own reaction to seeing this process of transformation live was amazement. Like a child at a magic show, I wondered where Tomlin had gone, since she disappeared into character so rapidly and so completely. Tomlin has said that this focused work helps her capture "the essence" of each character and that she prefers it to commenting on a character as stand-ups do (Martin 377). Richard Pryor explains the phenomenon, which he shares with Tomlin: "I mean, the characters we do literally take possession of us. ... I've never seen it happen to any other entertainers but Lily and me. You can see the physical change take place when she's working. It is eerie" (qtd. in Martin 375). To cultivate the energy that this transformation demands, Tomlin will often jump up or bend low during a performance. "When I squat down and jump a lot, it's to energize. Or punctuate. Sometimes I jump up and down to renew my energy in the middle of a performance. You find different sources of energy. If it doesn't come to you, you have to find it in yourself (qtd. in Robinson 187).

In her stage shows, simplicity of staging and costuming heighten and sustain this technique, marking a contrast between her neutrally costumed stage shows and the character costuming of her television shows. For example, in the stage show *Appearing Nightly!* (1977), Tomlin wears a simple blouse, pants, and pumps and transforms quickly from one character to another. She exudes a sense of complete physicality as she uses the strength and agility of her athletic body to move from one character to another. The stage is bare except for one stool and a box, both painted blue like her outfit. Sometimes there is a series of one-liners between sketches, possibly so Tomlin can physically recover and the audience can emotionally adjust before the next sketch. Each of the major pieces ends with a walk to the dark upstage area and then a reentry onto the lit stage to the applause of the audience. The simple staging allows Tomlin to become as many as four characters in one sketch. For example, in the Lud and Marie sketch, Tomlin plays Lud, Marie, the daughter, and the salesman. At one point she has Marie put her hand over Lud's mouth, which Tomlin achieves by putting her hand over her own mouth. Characters work in big, clean, single gestures, supplemented by simple sound effects.

Tomlin saw the actress Ruth Draper (1894–1956) as a model for her form (Robinson 187). Draper, who worked as a successful woman comic actress during the first half of the century, concentrated on women characters, always performed alone, and changed monologues rapidly from one character to another with accent and voice shifts. In staging she used only minimal props (shawls and stools) to assist in creating her world of characters. In a famous piece called "The Italian Lesson," Draper used the telephone as a device that continually intrudes on her Italian lesson, so that when she is finished with children, husband, lover, friends, and complex social arrangements for the day and evening, she has learned only one line of Dante. Tomlin pushed the model of the one-woman show much further, replacing Draper's physically reserved characters with a wide range of highly physicalized women. Whereas Draper drew on wealthy women characters almost exclusively, Tomlin/Wagner drew characters from all levels of society, with an emphasis on those without privilege. While the former's characters benefited unquestioningly from their high class status, the latter's lower class characters, like Tess and Crystal, challenge the hierarchy of power and money.

INFLUENCE OF LILY TOMLIN ON OTHER COMEDIANS

Lily Tomlin helped move comedy from the safety zone of pure entertainment to the more provocative place it now holds. Since few women comedians before her had taken committed stands as social commentators, her effect upon younger women comedians is incalculable. Gilda Radner, for example, said, "She's paving the way for other women like me who want to do comedy" (qtd. in Martin 367). But her effect was not just on younger comedians or on women. In his 1995 biography, *Pryor Convictions*, Richard Pryor describes the importance of working with Tomlin as a writer and actor on her two 1973 CBS comedy specials.

> She'd make me goofus from laughing so hard. Then she'd switch gears and inject a poignancy that made you think about the way you looked at the world. That shit was inspiring. It took comedy to a different level. I tried doing the same during a skit in which I played a junkie in a soul food cafe, someone trying to get both dignity and dinner (136).

Pryor is referring to a sketch called "Juke and Opal" which the network almost deleted from the show, because it dealt with his character strung out on methadone. Ready to sue over its removal, Tomlin won her battle to keep the piece. Richard Pryor went on to create his own comic waves by redefining the role of black comedians, rejecting the politer fare offered by Bill Cosby and making his own bold challenges to racism.

Tomlin's influence on younger comedians can be traced through the decades. Gilda Radner's 1978 show *Gilda Live*, and Whoopi Goldberg's 1984 one-woman show *The Spook Show*, both of which played on Broadway, have their one-woman show form in common with Tomlin's *Appearing Nitely!*. Goldberg's show includes a disabled woman character who, like Crystal in *Appearing Nitely!*, criticizes the society which has excluded her, but does so without *self-pity*. Roseanne credits Tomlin with providing an early model for her (*Who Makes You Laugh?*). Lorne Michaels, creator of *Saturday Night Live*, considered Tomlin "the progenitor of 'comedian's lib'" for establishing "a place where comedy is given more than one dimension, where jokes per se are abandoned" (qtd. in Dresner 182).

CONCLUSION: NEGATIVE EXEMPLAR AND LICENSED SPOKESPERSON

Mintz's definition of the role of the stand-up undergoes a significant shift in the work of Tomlin/Wagner. Whereas Diller becomes a clown, a negative exemplar, the object of ridicule, in order to have a mask behind which she could safely perform as licensed spokesperson, Tomlin, by contrast, fully fleshes out human characters in order to play out her role as licensed spokesperson. Tomlin/Wagner challenge middle-class complacency by presenting those who are marginalized by gender, poverty, disability, and age. Bolstered by their feminism, Tomlin/Wagner's role as licensed spokesperson becomes visible in depth and honesty in comparison to the more "invisible" satire of Diller. In this sense, Tomlin/Wagner reject Mintz's assignation of comedian as "negative exemplar" loser.

Tomlin/Wagner replace the role of negative exemplar with that of shaman, center of creativity, bearer of insight, artist, healer. In no way is this contrast between Diller and Tomlin more obvious than in the way they foreground their bodies. While Diller covers up and ridiculously costumes her figure, Tomlin uncovers her body so it can give birth to a new life and spirit. While Diller covers her body to avert the "male gaze," Tomlin uncovers her form to reveal her body's multitudinous incarnations. The male eye/I is not the primary gaze for which Tomlin's comedy is performed. Her characters, both men and women, show immense difference in class and attitude from each other, yet those who have identified most closely with the patriarchy (Ernestine, Mrs. Beasly, Suzie Sorority) are the most damaged. By contrast, those characters that break from the patriarchy into a freer individuality, like Tess, Crystal and Sister Boogie Woman, offer alternative roles for women in their independence of thought and spirit. Lily Tomlin and Jane Wagner's comedy models alternative routes for unfolding an adult life, routes that defy conventional expectations for women in roles as wives and mothers. In this sense, the dominance of the patriarchy in the '50s and '60s had an inhibiting effect on Diller's comedy, whereas the rise of feminism in the late '60s and '70s had a freeing effect on the Tomlin/Wagner comedy, a freedom that they extend to their audience as an alternative to the *status quo*.

An extraordinary effect of the collaboration of Lily Tomlin and Jane Wagner has been to communicate a rare depth of humanity in their unforgettable characters. As one reviewer remarked after watching a performance of *Search* in L.A. in 2003, "She's not showing off her extraordinary mimetic skills when she's morphing through the 12 characters of *Search*, she's showing us each other." As women's stand-up continues to develop through the decades, Roseanne returns to the "pure" standup of one comedian telling jokes in direct address to the audience. However, her inhabitation of the stand-up role once again shifts the paradigm of stand-up as negative exemplar and licensed spokesperson. By creating an angry and confrontive comedy, free of self-deprecation and challenging to the patriarchal order, Roseanne shows the influence of feminism and of the work of Tomlin/Wagner. Her work, which identified with the traditional roles of wife and mother, makes use of feminist stand-up to elevate that role. In her one-woman shows, her early stand-up, and in *Roseanne!*, her famous sitcom, Roseanne makes light of society's restrictions on women and loosens those boundaries through laughter.

Chapter Four

Roseanne
Fighting for Women's Comic Voice

> "Roseanne, you are going to be the one who breaks down the doors for Comedy and Women."
> Mitzi Shore of L.A.'s Comedy Store (qtd. in Barr 204)

AT 5'4", FEET PLANTED FIRMLY ON THE EARTH, LOUD, SLOPPY, AND foul-mouthed, Roseanne looks more like a woman ready to fight over a sale item in a bargain basement store than a leader in women's comedy. Nevertheless, through a crafty combination of an aggressive persona and a housewife theme, Roseanne's comedy has widened the boundaries for women comedians and has brought feminist themes into the mainstream. As she told Alan King in an interview: "The goddess of all creation said that it was about time that someone started talking about how us women have been overlooked. She asked me to go out there and do it" (Barr, interview).

By combining a feminist critique of the housewife role with a relentless targeting of male domination, Roseanne's comedy challenges America's view of gender relations and forefronts the working class. Her one-liners assert the triumphal attitude of woman as survivor:

> When my husband comes home at night, I figure if the kids are still alive, I've done my job (*The Roseanne Barr Show*).

Through brash attacks on gender roles, Roseanne takes the myths of motherhood and the idealization of women and sets them both spinning.

BIOGRAPHY

Born in 1952 in Salt Lake City, the comic grew up Jewish, but was culturally immersed in Mormonism. Though she celebrated Sabbath each week at the apartment of her grandmother, a Holocaust survivor, she and her mother also practiced Mormonism. As a child, Roseanne became a Mormon Youth Speaker and went around to churches speaking about her miraculous recovery from a facial paralysis. From these engagements, she learned the skill of moving people with speech (Barr 172). From her father, Leonard Barr, Roseanne learned the rewards of being funny. "We would always have contests, showdowns, and I would always win. Even if it was anti-male, anti-him, he would say, 'Good one'" (qtd. in Lahr 45). At age sixteen, Roseanne was struck by a car, the head ornament of which pierced her skull; she was subsequently institutionalized in a mental hospital for eight months. At the age of eighteen, she gave a baby up for adoption and took to the road (Lahr 45). Ending up in the small mountain community of Georgetown, Colorado, Roseanne met her first husband, Bill Pentland, a motel night clerk. They soon married, had three children, and moved to Denver where they lived in a 600 sq. ft. house.

In 1976, Roseanne began working part time as a window-dresser, making forty dollars a week, but then got a better job as a hostess/waitress at a Bennigan's restaurant. In 1980 she began to volunteer at the Woman to Woman Bookstore in Denver, educated herself by reading, and also joined the Woman's Collective, a politically active feminist group. Roseanne's brash persona can be traced back to her Bennigan's job, and her act's feminist content emerged from her bookstore experience. Because the Bennigan's customers found her "insult humor" so entertaining, they encouraged Roseanne to audition a stand-up act at The Comedy Shoppe in downtown Denver. In addition to doing comedy one night a week at that prestigious club, Roseanne began performing stand-up at The Mercury Cafe, Muddie's Coffee House, the Unitarian Church, and a strip club, Straite Johnson's (Barr 1-188).

Encouraged in these "funkier" venues by her friends from the bookstore, Roseanne began to develop material with a feminist edge. Sometimes she would appear in fishnet stockings and low cut tops, and then break into a feminist routine, playing with the contradiction between her image and her content. Because she offended some audience members, Roseanne claims she was banned from Denver's The Comedy Shoppe (Barr 191-2). To retaliate, she produced a women's comedy show entitled "Take Back the Mic" at the University of Colorado at Boulder, to complement the University's "Take Back the Night" anti-rape march (Lahr 47). Her program note read: "Roseanne Barr—Person of Ceremonies: an adorably angry/vicious comic, wife of years, mother of three, affectionately referred to as 'castrating bitch' by many male colleagues" (59). During this show, Roseanne strategically announced that she had been censored in Denver and used pressure from the press to help her remount Denver stages. By 1983 Roseanne was named the Queen of Denver Comedy, having won the Denver Laff-Off contest by beating out sixteen men (Marleah Leslie & Associates).

Confident from her Denver sweep, Roseanne auditioned in L.A. at Mitzi Shore's The Comedy Store, and after her six minutes in Showcase, Shore sent

Roseanne 55

Roseanne upstairs for twenty minutes in the Main Room. That night Mitzi Shore hired Roseanne to appear in George Schlatter's ABC Special, "Funny," in a segment about women comics (Marleah Leslie & Associates 2). As a result of being seen during rehearsal for "Funny" by Jim McCowley, Talent Coordinator of "The Tonight Show," Roseanne made her first appearance with Johnny Carson the following Friday (2). She moved to L. A. in 1985 and in 1986 was a guest on the 26th Anniversary Special of "The Tonight Show" (Celebrity Bio).

In 1987 Roseanne taped her first stand-up HBO special, *The Roseanne Barr Show*, which she wrote with Bill Pentland, her husband at that time, and Rocco Urbisci, the show's director. The show features stand-up comedy in a living room setting where the main character, Roseanne, leaves the stage frequently to attend to her family, fighting in a trailer in the parking lot. (Of note is the fact that Tom Arnold, soon to be Roseanne's second husband, played the role of the father of the fictional family.) This comedy special won an ACE Award (cable's Emmy) for Best Female Comedy and another for Best HBO Special (Celebrity Bio). It became her pilot to the networks to pitch an idea for the television sitcom *Roseanne!*, which first aired on ABC in October of 1988. In 1989, Harper and Row published her first book, *Roseanne: My Life as a Woman*, and in 1992 Ballantine Books published her second book, *Roseanne: My Lives*. Roseanne has five children and has been divorced three times.

Roseanne has received many awards for her television show *Roseanne!*, including the 1993 Golden Globe award for Best Actress in a Comedy Series and an Emmy in acting. In 1990 she won two People's Choice Awards: Favorite All-Around Female Television Performer and Favorite All-Around Female Entertainer. Two American Comedy Awards came her way in 1988: Funniest Female Performer in a television series and Funniest Stand-up Comic (Marleah Leslie & Associates).

After the last episode of her long-running sitcom, *Roseanne!* (1988–1997), Roseanne went on to New York to play a short run in *The Wizard of Oz*—as the wicked witch. The play ran for one month from May 7 through June 1 in Madison Square Garden, but though the play ended, the Roseanne drama continued. Roseanne's television talk show, *The Roseanne Show*, lasted from 1998–2000, but finally it could not compete at the time with *The Oprah Winfrey Show* or *The Rosie O'Donnell Show*. In 1998 she also divorced her third husband, Ben Thomas, who had been her driver and with whom she had a son.[1]

By 2003, Roseanne Barr had gone back to her birth name "Barr" and had two television projects. In August, she starred on a reality/comedy show, *The Real Roseanne,* and in September she began to host a celebrity cooking show, *Domestic Goddess*, which was guaranteed for thirteen episodes. In preparation for the reality show, Roseanne told reporters that she was working on being nicer and that the reality show would prove it. In an article for *Time* entitled, "A Rose Without Thorns?," Roseanne said she's showing herself as "the best example of a really horrible person who has changed" (61).

Roseanne's adjustments to losing her sitcom and the bright spotlight were painful for some to watch. For example, when she announced in 2000, after losing seventy-five pounds, that she was negotiating with *Playboy* for a spread, a *Time* report read, "Oh, Please, Dear God, No" (85). In a television interview for *The View* in August, 2003, Roseanne pitched her new *Roseanne Reality Show*, but then went on to pitch her new "nice" personality: "As soon as I started being nice, this whole thing overtook me, and I wanted to have sex.... I swear to God I don't have mean bone in my body." Persuasive as a "nice" person or not, it is clear that Roseanne's brazen housewife role in her stand-up and in her television sitcom *Roseanne!* broke new ground for women and comedy.

ROSEANNE AS NEGATIVE EXEMPLAR: NASTY, BRUTISH, AND SHORT

At first glance, Roseanne fits well into Lawrence Mintz's definition of the comedian as "negative exemplar" ("New Wave" 1). As a "negative model"—too short, too loud, too big, too ethnic—Roseanne embodies everything the idealized woman is not supposed to be. On closer examination, however, Roseanne's persona folds the role of comic as negative model into its reverse, that of comic as positive model. Validating a different body shape, a working-class background, the life of a housewife, and an outspokenness for her version of the truth, Roseanne's persona stands in defiance of middle class restrictions on women. As John Lahr of *The New Yorker* suggests: "Roseanne's rejection of manners and of clean language is both a critique of and a revenge on the decorum of patriarchy, which assures women collude in their own destruction" (47).

Whereas the classic clown presents himself as an object of ridicule so that the audience finds cohesion in its group mockery at "the other," Roseanne deliberately presents herself as "the other" in order to validate "otherness" and to cast doubt on the shallowness of the acceptable. While Roseanne stood firmly in her flat shoes, chomped on her gum, and slaughtered grammar, she spoke her mind freely without a trace of self-deprecation or intimidation. Refusing to fulfill the expectations that a woman have a Barbie Doll figure, a correct education, a polite demeanor, an apolitical mind, and an obsession with her own attractiveness, Roseanne's early "nasty, brutish, and short" image becomes her platform, her medium, her message.

NASTY

Rejecting the standard that women be polite and respectful, Roseanne thrives on insult humor for its shocking blast of truth: "I mean, you may marry the man of your dreams, but fifteen years later, you're married to a reclining chair that burps" (*The Roseanne Barr Show*). On her night shift as a waitress at

Bennigan's, Roseanne had honed this humor as a weapon against rudeness and sexual innuendo. "One day something just snapped, and I talked back to them. This man said, 'Bring me one of these, honey.' I turned around and I said, 'Don't call me honey, you fuckin' pig.' He just started laughing—good thing" (Barr 183). Testing her limits in this style, she found that she was good at it, and that it drew more customers to Bennigan's. "I'd say, 'These drinks are gonna be six bucks, and it'll cost you three more to have me take 'em off the tray and put 'em on the table.' Soon people were coming in just to be insulted by me" (qtd. in Dworkin 109).

Although Roseanne did not invent insult humor, she gave it a feminist dimension. Henny Youngman's wife jokes defined his style, but his content was incidental and disconnected. While the insult humor of a comedian like Don Rickles tended to be based on personal attack, Roseanne's insult humor turned on gender inequities. Typically, Don Rickles would blast whoever was sitting next to him, as in this example of Rickles to Johnny Carson: "Hi, dum-dum," he said addressing Johnny. "Where's it say you butt in, dummy? That's it; laugh it up. You're making fifty million a year, and your parents are home in Nebraska eating locust for dinner" (qtd. in Keough 195). Roseanne's insult was usually aimed at her male target. "I thank God for creating gay men, because if it wasn't for gay men us fat women would have no one to dance with" (*The Roseanne Barr Show*). Thus, Roseanne's comedy responded to the audience's fascination with her aggressiveness, an attraction akin to the allure of handling a poisonous snake.

BRUTISH

Defying the expectation that women be refined, quiet and educated, Roseanne wore her working-class roots as a badge of honor. Of the year 1980, before she began to do stand-up, Roseanne said: "I had found my voice. No longer wishing to speak in academic language, or even in a feminist language, because it all seemed dead to me, I began to speak as a working-class woman who is a mother. This was the language that all the women on the street spoke" (Barr 18). To manifest her working class origins as a distinction of her comedy, Roseanne never elevated her roots or dressed them up, refusing, for example, to "clean up" her grammar:

> Don't never read any of those books by experts. They don't never have kids either. They say things like, "Don't ever hit your kids in anger." Think about that. When would be a good time to hit them? When you're feeling real festive? (*The Roseanne Barr Show*).

In this respect, Roseanne shows the influence of another of her models, Moms Mabley, who shuffled on stage in men's shoes, an old hat and dress, and spoke in her working class idiom. In objecting to constrictions on her life, Moms Mabley said of the old man her father picked out for her husband:

> His shadow weighed more than he did. He was so ugly, he hurt my feelings. He got out of breath threading a needle.... I thought he never would die.... I know he's dead, because I had him cremated. I determined that he should get hot one time (*Moms Mabley On Stage*).

Like Moms, Roseanne's early stand-up takes pride in dealing with the problems of daily life under circumstances of strained finances and few luxuries. Roseanne wants her comedy to challenge middle-class liberal mediocrity, including academic feminism, which she considers harmful to women and completely out of touch with the American people (Lahr 58). By maintaining her gum chewing, overweight and loud-mouthed persona, Roseanne was not simply representing "the little woman," but elevating the daily lives of the working class people. With a comedy that targeted a television audience member who was more likely a woman on welfare than a college-educated woman, Roseanne could say things like:

> ... the husband thinks that the wife knows where everything is, huh? Like they think the uterus is a tracking device. He comes in: "Hey, Roseanne! Roseanne! Do we have any Cheetos left?" Like he can't go over and lift up that sofa cushion himself? (*The Roseanne Barr Show*).

Even though the joke makes fun of men, it also makes fun of the housewife role and laughs off the shabby circumstances of the working class home. Roseanne knew she was responding to a need in the country: "At first, I think I stood for all the latent energy and talent that resides in ordinary folks living ordinary lives of quiet desperation in better trailer parks everywhere" (Arnold 218). Her dad had told her, "Comedy ... is funniest when it's about speaking up for the little man and killing sacred cows" (qtd. in Barr 66). As a child, a Jew displaced on a Mormon landscape, Roseanne learned how to champion the underdog. (Her grandparents housed survivors of the Nazi war camps in a tenement where Roseanne's family first lived) (31). In some of her jokes, Roseanne drew on both her Jewish roots and her working class background, as in this description of her first wedding to a gentile. "For my family he crushed a beer can under his foot. For his family I pretended I was a virgin" (*The Roseanne Barr Show*).

Many criticized Roseanne for crossing the line of the culturally acceptable when she butchered "The National Anthem," grabbed her crotch, and spat at a Padres game in 1990. According to a *People Weekly* report, President Bush called the incident "a disgrace" and Secretary of State Jim Baker described it as "disgusting." The event triggered over two thousand fan complaints by phone. Roseanne reported that though she can't sing, she thought she would be well received by the fans. According to Roseanne, the players in the dugout had suggested the crotch grabbing and spitting as a joke (Schindehette 44). When many people were offended, Roseanne backed off, and the popularity of her sitcom ultimately let the incident recede to the background. The baseball game incident did not stand alone, however. *People Weekly* also reported that the year before Roseanne and Tom Arnold had "mooned" a crowd at the Oakland Alameda County Coliseum when they were displeased with the score of the first game (44). In an appearance on the nationally televised *Comic Relief* in 1987, Roseanne appeared in a mink coat and diamond earrings, saying she would wear them until every homeless person was fed. Roseanne admitted that as she developed her iconoclastic persona for her comedy, she sometimes went too far. As she told the *People Weekly* reporter, "I sometimes get what I think is a good idea, but my judgment is wrong" (44).

Short

In defiance of conventional beauty, Roseanne's early stand-up asserts her own body image as a new possibility for women: "I think people just have sex because they cannot afford good food" (*The Roseanne Barr Show*). Making light of her own heaviness, Roseanne shows the influence of Totie Fields (born 1931), a stand-up performing in the 1960s and '70s, who she claims as an inspiration. In one routine, Totie stood on the stage with her arms extended, showing flab loosely hanging from her upper arms. "I am a firm believer in exercise. That's how I stay firm. Look how thin my fingers are" (qtd. in *Who Makes You Laugh?*). Unlike Totie Fields, though, Roseanne never makes fun of herself, but instead targets a culture that wants all women thin. Of Hollywood's body fascists, she said, "People out here are rude to the fat. I went into a store looking for something, 'Do you have anything to make me look thinner?' The girl says, 'How's about a month in Bangladesh?' So I told her, 'Hey, I eat the same amount of food you eat, I just don't puke when I'm done'" (*The Roseanne Barr Show*).

Roseanne attacks the mystique of diets and the pressures of guilt women place on themselves. She begins this routine by showing how women kid themselves about calories, and ends it:

> You're not gonna lose no weight. Here's the key. Just be fat and shut up, and if you're thin, FUCK YOU! (*The Roseanne Barr Show*).

Roseanne exaggerated her unglamorous and working class look to define her comic persona, even though she was under pressure to make her stage image conform to norms of attractiveness. After seeing her early act at a Denver comedy club, Diane Ford, a professional woman comic from L.A., said to Roseanne: "You cannot look fat and be a woman comic. People will hear it easier from you if you are beautiful, well kept, and professional than if you are kind of slobbed out" (qtd. in Barr 189).

In the 1980s, Roseanne did change from tight clothes to loose fitting tunics, but she had refused to give up her gum chewing, flat shoes, bad grammar, and colorful language.

In the '90s Roseanne's plastic surgeries and continuous diets compromised for some people her position as champion of alternative body images for women. Of these surgeries, critic Phillip Auslander suggests, "She has sacrificed much of the edge that originally gave her stand-up its pith and power" (336). Her scream of outrage against the pressure on women for standard beauty lost some volume when she subjected her own body to these pressures. However, after a stomach operation Roseanne claimed that she has been able to be more accepting of her big and full body type: "I feel that I have been able to reverse the years of damage to my physical being and my self-esteem. After forty-one years, I finally feel *no shame* or disgust looking at myself in a mirror—I am a big, round, normal-shaped woman, with scars" (Arnold 231).

ROSEANNE AS LICENSED SPOKESPERSON

Roseanne embraces her role as licensed spokesperson, seizing the unique opportunities stand-up offers a woman. She recognized in it "a place, perhaps the only place where a woman can speak as a woman, as a stranger in a strange land, as part of a group that defined itself in its own view, with its own words in a manner that seemed to heal, instead of wound" (Barr 168). Her passion on this point has the fervor of religious zeal. Roseanne remembers that the first time she went on stage she felt "chilled and free and redeemed. What excited me, finally, was the thought of a woman, any woman, standing up and saying NO..." (Barr 168).

Clearly aligned with the social commentary of the "New Wave" comedians, and influenced by the feminist comedy of Lily Tomlin, Roseanne considered Richard Pryor "the greatest comedian who ever lived" (qtd. in *Who Makes You Laugh*). Roseanne used Richard Pryor's truth telling on racial issues as her model for truth telling on women's issues: "I knew that he was inside the stereotype and fighting against it, that he was going to blow it up from the inside. I got that immediately. I thought, by God, I'm going to do the same thing being a woman" (qtd. in Lahr 45). Just as Pryor broke through to a deeper level of truth telling in racial issues, Roseanne broke through to another level of truth telling about women's experience. When she found the language to make it both funny and provocative, that language was angry.

ROSEANNE'S FEM RAGE

Roseanne became a one-woman volcano erupting through the pressures that had held her down. Because women are socialized against anger, Roseanne's comedy was fathoming new depths, punching out a degree of aggression never before seen in a woman comic. Her discourse on her own work is dominated with fight and death images: "People will laugh and think you're an asshole if they want to, but you're still sayin' it, so therefore it was possible to say it without getting killed" (Barr

200-1). Roseanne pictures herself as always rising to the fight, or never "taking it."

> I think that's what makes me a bit different from other women. Because I'll beat the shit out of them [men], and not just verbally. I'm not opposed to violence. In fact, I think it's great. I think women should be more violent, kill more of their husbands. I like the fight. If people are comin' at you, you don't just sit there and lay down (qtd. in Lahr 58).

In her second television comedy special, Roseanne used her attraction to violence in a story about a serial killer, Mrs. Polente, who ran a boarding house:

> She killed these seven guys and she hacked their bodies to bits and she buried them out in her garden, and she stole their social security checks and all this type of shit. Of course, I'd like to go out on a limb and say, I am not for that. But you can sort of understand it, she's on a limited income (*Roseanne: Live from Trump Tower*).

In real life, Roseanne claims she had to become her angry persona, in order to successfully fight for her ideas on the television show, *Roseanne!* (1988-1997). In a somewhat prophetic piece for her first HBO comedy special, *The Roseanne Barr Show*, she advertised a product called "Fem Rage" that was designed to help women be more aggressive at work. In the ad Roseanne plays a female worker in a nuclear lab who is rebuked by her male boss when she politely tells him that they are on the verge of a nuclear melt down. "When I want your opinion I'll give it to you," responds the boss. Upset at not being liked, worker Roseanne asks her female colleagues what to do. One tells her, "Honey, let me tell you what we do when we're feeling overly submissive. [Holding up a bottle] Try Fem Rage! For that one time of month when you're allowed to be yourself. It counteracts that learned feminine response." After taking the product, Roseanne pushes her boss out of the way and saves the world. When the head of the plant asks, "Who saved the world?" the male boss steps forward to take credit, but Roseanne stares him back and walks forward, proudly announcing "I did." "Thank you, honey," the head answers. The ad is a banner for Roseanne's value system: Be polite and nice and you get trampled; be assertive and save the world.

Roseanne consumed large doses of "Fem Rage" to bring her television show up to her high standards of comedy writing. One of her complaints at the beginning of production of *Roseanne!* was that the writers were conventionalizing her ideas: "They were eviscerating my show, goddammit, they were Osterizing it into the pastel puree that had been spread over the networks for too long now, the same unsatisfying, tasteless, colorless (forget odorless—it stunk) polenta of sitcoms that I couldn't stomach" (Arnold 91-2).

Her passionate and aggressive personality made production of her television show a battleground (234). Roseanne was on the warpath against family sitcoms with weak female roles, no ideological substance, and the glamorization of the middle class. She fought for a strong female character, for a story line that dealt with real family problems told in a working class language. "In my show, the Woman is no longer a victim, but in control of her own mind. I wanted to make family sitcoms as we know them obsolete" (234).

When ABC accepted her special *The Roseanne Barr Show* as a pilot for the television show *Roseanne!* she was first cast in role of the sister, not the main character she had created. Creative control of the show was in the hands of head writer, Matt Williams. A breaking point between the two came when Roseanne was asked in a love scene to say this line to her television husband, John Goodman: "You are my equal in bed, but that's it." Roseanne refused to say the line, would not move off the rehearsal bed, and forced the cameras to go black during the taping. After a day and a half of no work, the line was cut and Roseanne had begun to take creative control of her product, eventually earning (in the 1996–7 season) over a million dollars per episode (Lahr 42).

The degree of aggression needed to maintain her show according to her own vision created a unique dynamic between Roseanne's stand-up roles as licensed spokesperson and negative exemplar, where the roles overlapped and became inseparable. She was learning, as producer of her show and a public personality, that her own personality needed to take on the characteristics of her Hobbesian "nasty, brutish, and short" stage character. An example of this is the finale of her second comedy special (1993). In a rebuttal to Arsenio Hall, a late night talk show host who had been mocking her for being fat, she appears to have no persona, but to talk unmasked from her heart. As the piece reaches its climax, this unmasking of self creates a vulnerability combined with a warrior's fierceness. She begins by giving a simple biography, saying that she's 37 years old, has four kids, is Jewish, and was raised in Salt Lake City, among Mormons. She goes on to tell that her dad sold crucifixes door to door to Mexicans and that when she was seven she fell down, bit off her lip, and had to have it sewn back on. She continues:

> When I was sixteen I got hit by a car, got my head impaled on the hood ornament, my legs shot thirty feet; got pregnant the first time I ever had sex. My parents made me give the kid up for adoption; I found her 18 years later, after her face was splashed across the front page of *The National Enquirer*. Spent eight months in a state institution, a mental institution, hitch hiked across the country three times, by myself, with hepatitis, lived in a car, a cabin, and a cave, married a guy just because he had a fuckin' bathtub, had three more kids. He treated me like shit every day for sixteen years, and when I finally got the guts to dump that son of a bitch, I have to pay him half the money I make for the rest of my god damn life. Arsenio, FUCK WITH ME!
> (*Roseanne: Live From Trump Tower*).

The imagery of much of her comedy centers on breaking out of imprisoning systems that entrap both women and men. In the following quotation, it is clear that she sees her job as liberating women from these systems; anger is her means of breaking out. "I think of my mother, I think of all the women in the nuthouse, I think of all the women from all time. And I go, 'Hey I will not be insulted anymore. I will not hate myself anymore. There is no way to beat me, because I am so pissed'" (qtd. in Dworkin 206). Often her anger is that of a beast pent up in a cage, as in the following piece about her 15th wedding anniversary, where she compares marriage to "captivity":

> When I got done admiring my new Dust Buster, I thought back to the early years of our marriage. I have three children. I breed well in captivity (*The Roseanne Barr Show*).

Roseanne especially makes fun of married women who collude in their own subjugation:

> [using a light airy voice] Girls, it's really nice seeing you, but I really have to get going because this is the second night in a row that Tom let me stay out late. [back to her own voice] Oh, uh, huh. He let you stay out late. He LET you stay out late. He LEEEEEETTTTT YOU stay out late (*Roseanne: Live From Trump Tower*).

Not only did she strip down the romantic myths that kept power roles in place, Roseanne also sought to expose the emptiness of some of the gender games between men and women:

> On my husband's birthday I say the things to build up his ego. "Your mother's the most interesting person I ever met" (*Roseanne: Live From Trump Tower*).

Roseanne continually urges women to a greater state of awareness where they see their own willing participation in sexism. In the following routine, Roseanne questions the ultimate goals of flirtation, comparing it to the capitalist system of acquisition:

> Hey, ladies, I've tried smelling like a peach, a wildflower, fruited hibiscus, but it didn't get me shit. Well, now there's a feminine deodorant spray, invented by a gynecologist, guaranteed to drive men mad, it will turn them into raging animals that will fight to the death to get next to you 'cause it smells like . . . money" (Barr, *My Life as a Woman* 198).

With great consistency, Roseanne deflates sexist assumptions as in the following case when she challenges men for assuming superiority they have not earned.

> You do only two things better than us women. One is map reading. Let's give credit where credit is due. Only the male mind could conceive of one inch as a hundred miles (*The Roseanne Barr Show*).

Roseanne builds solidarity with women in her audience by engaging in a direct dialogue with them about their husbands. With men also listening, her dialogue often challenges the patriarchal system where it fails both genders. Rather than repel the men in her audience, as predicted by her agents and advisors, Roseanne was winning them over.

> The thing was, once they started laughing, they loved it. Surprisingly, men loved my act—as raunchy as it was—I expected it to be threatening and overpowering as prophesied, but they liked it. They loved jokes about how stupid they were. They loved it not so much because it was the truth but because, as Santayana once said, the only true dignity of man is his capacity to despise himself. Or maybe it's all that dominatrix-whore thing they got going, I don't know. Maybe I just tapped into some weird guy-type Zeitgeist (Barr 55).

Had something changed in the American culture so that men could now tolerate public ridicule from women? Why did men laugh at routines like the following, which clearly put them down?

> A lot of men are impotent and it's very sad. How many of you are impotent? [no hands go up] I see. Can't get your arms up either? (*The Roseanne Barr Show*).

In her performance style, Roseanne had a friendly tone under her insult humor, a tone that included men. Often, if she addressed women, she nodded to the men and laughingly said something like, "You guys know you do that, don't you?" Nonetheless, even though it includes men, her comedy announces that the time for standing up to them has arrived.

A search of the '80s national scene elicits two cultural currents which helped push Roseanne's humor forward to popularity: 1) the advances in the lives of women, 2) the blows to the middle class created by Reaganomics. Roseanne's was a woman's comic voice in a swelling sea of women's voices, and the '80s provided a supportive cultural context. Even though Phyllis Schlafly was gearing up her anti-feminist backlash, and the Equal Rights Amendment had been defeated, the 1980s marked significant advances for women in many fields (Trager 664–700). On the political front Indira Gandhi and Margaret Thatcher were serving as heads of state. In 1984 Geraldine Ferraro became the first American woman nominated by a major party to run for Vice President. Jean Kirkpatrick became the U.S. Representative to the United Nations; Sandra Day O'Connor became the first woman justice to the

Supreme Court; Sally Ride became the first U.S. woman to go into space. Women were gaining prominence in many fields: Barbara McClintock won the Nobel Prize for physiology/medicine (1983), Alice Walker won the Pulitzer Prize for her novel *The Color Purple* (1982), Maya Ying Lin, an architect student at Yale, designed the impressive Viet Nam Memorial in Washington, D.C. Women playwrights Marsha Norman, Beth Henley and Wendy Wasserstein were succeeding on Broadway. Wasserstein was the first female playwright to win the Tony Award for Best Play with *The Heidi Chronicles* (1989); she also won the Pulitzer Prize with this play. The cultural wind was blowing in the direction of Roseanne's themes. "Women rule the world," said Bob Dylan in a *Rolling Stone* interview in June, 1984. Dylan continued, "No man has ever done anything that a woman either hasn't allowed him to do or encouraged him to do" (qtd. in Trager 682).

More subtly, Roseanne's working class comedy arose at a time when, according to many economic analysts, the middle class was taking a beating. In its simplest terms, Reaganomics left the rich richer and the poor poorer, even though its intention was to stimulate the economy to "trickle down" to all economic levels (Schaller 26–7). In fact, Reagan's supply side economics resulted in huge tax cuts for the wealthy and an increase in the visible poor. Robert Reich reported that, between 1975 and 1985, one out of three Americans fell below the poverty line at least once (174), many of these being women and children (Schaller 79). In this shifting economic sea, the middle class worker watched the wealthy flaunt their new prosperity, and the poor crowd the streets as the new homeless. The working class had reason to be threatened. In this economic context, Roseanne's bold comedy would appeal not only as a diversion, but as a confidence booster, since it sympathetically positioned the working class. The following routine, for example, makes light of living in a trailer:

> ... It's kind of a little bit embarrassing to live in mobile home, huh? Yeah, like you can get a flat tire on your house. Now you're in bed. "Honey, is the door closed? Are the windows shut? Is the brake set?" (*The Roseanne Barr Show*).

This routine demonstrates a unique feature of Roseanne's stand-up comedy, one held by few other women comedians—a solidarity with the working class. Even though Roseanne developed her comedy at a time when its unique themes had sympathetic listeners, she did not depend on the mood of the country to base her comedy. For that, she gave her attention to words and their rhythms.

LANGUAGE/CRAFT

Roseanne's act depends not only on her unique persona and themes, but also on her distinct language. In the end, her routine is not ideology but entertainment; it elicits laughter through the deliberate placement of language and manipulation of time. Though her early Denver stand-up was highly radical, Roseanne abandoned academic language in favor of a more proletarian speech. What appeared to be ungrammatical patter was actually carefully honed word arrangements, particularly attuned to the effects of verbal rhythms, as in this opening of her 1986 show:

> I never get out of the house, I never go no place, I never have no fun, ever, ever, 'cause I'm a housewife. I hate that word, I want to be called, "Domestic Goddess" (*The Roseanne Barr Show*).

The repetition of "never" and "ever" sends the piece on a verbal roll, screaming in frustration for a way out, which is achieved in the counterpoise of the words "housewife" and "Domestic Goddess." As a whole, the rhythm announces the need for the housewife to run away and find an escape from her drudgery. Through economy and rhythm manipulation the piece gives the audience the experience of the speaker, thus drawing them into the idea of the piece.

Roseanne's commitment to simple and direct speech attracts her to street language, "I love the word 'fuck'... It's a verb, a noun, everything, and it's just infused with intense feeling and passion, you know, negative and positive. And women aren't supposed to say it, so I try to say it as much as I can" (qtd in Lahr 47). Though Roseanne's vulgar speech has drawn considerable attention, her sensitivity to sound has been almost ignored. As a housewife she wrote poetry and stashed it into Hefty bags; she read Dylan Thomas and Gertrude Stein. As a stand-up, she used the "jazz of words" to invigorate her comedy.

Her jokes vary in length and often contain lists of sounds in words that help physicalize their meaning, such as this announcement (in her first HBO special) of a housewife's crisis:

> Nov. 3, 1981, it's my birthday, I'm doing all that regular housewife stuff like cookin', curtainin', dustin', pot roast, scourin' out the tub with this non-abrasive cleanser, and all of sudden I get this regular reality alert, where your brain falls out of your head and falls on the floor. I love my husband, I love my kids, but I need something else.... I'm two days past happy (*The Roseanne Barr Show*).

The rhythm of "cookin', curtainin', dustin', pot roast, scourin' out the tub" invites the listener into the housewife's empty-headed frenzy. By contrast, the words "your brain falls out of your head and falls on the floor" end the frenzy with a thunk and announce the redirection of verbal and emotional energy.

In her Denver days, Roseanne occasionally performed stand-up at a jazz club. "It did something to my consciousness as a comedian. The rhythms got in my brain and shook loose the convention, like dirt off a radish root—it got me into the music of talk" (Barr 55). In the following piece, Roseanne makes a sharp shift of rhythm, beginning with a casual conversation tone:

> How come we do that? How come I'm always saying, "God, I'm no good at math." "God, I can't balance a check book, I'm no good with numbers." Then I notice, when I go shopping, I turn into a math wizard (*Roseanne: Live From Trump Tower*).

At this point, Roseanne computes out loud in a quick tempo, but her concentration and confidence assure accuracy.

> ... that dress is $42.00; 1/3 off 42 that's $14.00. That's $28.00 with 6 1/2% sales tax; God, I wish they would have bought this dress in Minnesota-they have no sales tax there. That's $1.72. So the total cost of this dress is $29.72. All right. Um, umm (*Roseanne: Live From Trump Tower*).

This manipulation of language demonstrates Roseanne's mastery of her delivery. "You can be a real witty bastard in writing and people will chuckle. But stand-up happens at the speed of light. The material has to work in delivery" (Barr 47). Roseanne learned how to pare an idea down to get the big laugh. "I'd get an idea, like, say, my husband wants me to be more aggressive in bed. Then I'd just write about it in my notebook, pages and pages, just to get one joke, kind of the way it takes a whole bunch of tree sap to make one jar of syrup" (47). In its final form the following joke turns on a tight premise, a hook, and a punchline:

> The *premise*: He comes in and he says, "Roseanne, why don't you try to be more aggressive in bed?"
> The *hook*: So, I thought about it and the other night, we're lying there and he reaches for me,
> The *punchline*: and I said, [screaming] "NOOOOOOOO!" (*Roseanne: Live From Trump Tower*).

The necessity to keep jokes economical challenged Roseanne: "I learned so much from stand-up, I learned discipline which I'd never had in my life, I learned about language, communication, and writing" (Barr 208). Even though she respected economy, she never exclusively followed a joke formula, using many stories and different length narratives to complete her act. In critiquing a library book on stand-up, which suggested a three part mathematical formula for comedy, Roseanne said, "This is the kind of comedy I do not do. What I do is based on a brand new theory that we women have our own way of thinking, different from the way men think, and way different from the way they think we think" (197). She found a form to fit her content.

Roseanne brought a high standard of writing to her television show, *Roseanne!* Kevin Abbot, one of her show's writers, told John Lahr, "The reason the show's been good over the years is that the writers are afraid to bring crap to the table" (58). Lahr's article implies that Roseanne used a reign of terror to hold her writers in line (58). But she writes in *My Lives* that the fight for her vision was worth it:

> I became a fighter, a soldier, in 1980. I wanted to bring to the stage, to the media, and to my own life, the idea of a woman who was strong and brave, sly and mouthy. I created a television show called "Roseanne," which became the battleground of and for myself. To allow for the freedom, the creative control, and the growth of this show, I had to become as strong and brave, sly, and mouthy as that woman on TV (Arnold 235).

Has Roseanne broken down the doors of comedy for women? Why did Mitzi Shore, who had bolstered the career of so many famous comedians, tap this "nasty, brutish, and short" one as the revolutionary leader for women and comedy? During her *Roseanne!* show years, working as a negative exemplar, Roseanne completely rejected the idealization of women and held out her own persona as a positive model which opposed the norm. Unfettered in her stand-up from the imposed male standard for female beauty and behavior, Roseanne unleashed her anger at the double standard, and in contrast to the positive humanism of Tomlin/Wagner, her comedy unabashedly attacks the patriarchy and urges change. Roseanne holds the mic with pleasure, enjoying the phallocentric echoes of her dominant position on stage, and then insults men for their insensitivity to women. Roseanne moves the boundary of "other" by foregrounding the working class and reclaiming the role of wife and mother for feminism.

Even though she moved away from her working class subject in the years following her sitcom, Roseanne nonetheless deserves credit for what she was able to accomplish with her sitcom and with her stand-up career. No other comedian combined the normality of the housewife with the outrageous aggression of Roseanne. By developing a heightened working class persona, she placed on center stage blue-collar values that opposed the elitism of comedy and found humor in the everyday life of common people. She has been like a kamikaze pilot, with her eye fiercely on her target, ready to sacrifice everything for an explosion of laughter.

Roseanne was culturally poised in the '80s and '90s to make a difference in the gender pattern articulated by Virginia Woolf in *A Room of One's Own*:

"Women have served for centuries as looking-glasses possessing the magic and delicious power of reflecting the figure of man as twice its natural size. Without that power probably the earth would still be swamp and jungle" (35). Roseanne's comedy announced that the time had come for women to stop boosting men's egos at the expense of their own; it urged women to find the courage to look in their own mirrors and see themselves as full sized.

Because Roseanne was such a successful negative exemplar, it has been difficult for her to alter that role and to be taken seriously for her self-proclaimed personal reforms toward gentleness. Her plastic surgeries, diets, and personal wealth have somewhat buried the old Roseanne. Her cultivation of "niceness" was the last straw for many. What woman, if not Roseanne, could Americans depend upon to be nasty? America in the late '80s and '90s had been ready for a full-figured woman to champion the working class. It was less ready in the late '90s and 2000s to buy another nice pretty face. Apart from her personal reforms, successful and not, Roseanne continued to be a talented woman who could generate genuine humor. In a 2001 article in *Esquire* entitled "I've Learned," she demonstrates that she has not lost her bite: "The hardest thing I ever learned about being a wife was that I'm not the husband." Roseanne's comedy centered on blasting out truths that most people held private. In this process, she found freedom from the tyranny of shame. In the *Esquire* article she says she also learned: "You are as sick as your secrets." Although many would have preferred that Roseanne stay "nasty, brutish, and short," her comic achievement speaks for itself. The success of her show *Roseanne!* made possible shows with other female comedians including Margaret Cho and Ellen DeGeneres. *Roseanne!* presented a finely-nuanced working class family in which most families could see themselves. Whatever the complaints have been about Roseanne's self-presentation, few deny that she is funny. As Roseanne said in the *Esquire* article: "You can't refute comedy. It's a physical response in the body and in the mind. It comes and it snatches you up and makes you dance."

Chapter Five

Women's Comedy on the Stage
The Search for Signs of Intelligent Life in the Universe, by Jane Wagner

WHEN IN *A ROOM OF ONE'S OWN* VIRGINIA WOOLF ASKS, "WHAT if Shakespeare had a sister?" Woolf reaches back through layers of cultural history to locate reasons why so little literary work by women has come down through the centuries. That imaginary sister, Judith, was as equally talented and ambitious as her brother, but when she reached London, she met only scorn and rejection. To help Woolf understand the particular "maleness" of the English literary heritage, she concluded that for centuries, artistic ambition in a woman was considered not only out of place and purposeless, but it was also regarded as utterly contemptuous of the dominant society. In this investigation of women in solo comedy performance in America, it becomes evident that Woolf's observations about women's ambition also apply to women in comedy. Women's comedic ambition has met with considerable resistance, particularly in Phyllis Diller's early days in the '50s and '60s. Despite the presence of a growing number of famous female stand-ups, many contemporary stand-ups assert that men's stand-up commands more respect than women's (*Wisecracks*). Because of this cultural resistance to women's comedy, I have argued for the significance of comedians like Lily Tomlin and Roseanne, who have by their skill and style expanded the field for women.

Expanding upon the work of Nancy Walker (*A Very Serious Thing* 7, 8), a series of questions could be addressed concerning women in solo performance: What if women were free to use their full intellectual capacity in creating and expressing their humor? What if women's lives were accepted as equally important as men's lives and honored for their differences? If the status of women was equal to the status of men, how would that affect their humor? To the uniquely human behavior of creating laughter, what do women writers and performers contribute? What portrait of America do women comedians paint?

As an example of what women could produce given total freedom to develop their talent for comedy, I propose Jane Wagner's play *The Search for Signs of Intelligent Life in the Universe*. Fiercely intelligent, keenly aware of political and social nuances in the dominant culture, it portrays a variety of women's lives, presenting these lives as equal in status and importance to men's. Written by a lesbian, it is outside what Lynda Hart refers to as "a masculine imagery that passes as *the* symbolic order" (2), but its frankly feminist tone neither preaches nor exhorts. Rather, the play painfully critiques the society of the 1980s, exposing its shallowness and misdirections.

Search represents a unique stage in the collaboration between Wagner and Tomlin because, unlike previous work, credit for the writing goes entirely to Wagner. The play evidences her particular intelligence, which has the ability in Tomlin's words to be: "funny, satiric, passionate, emotional and poetic" (qtd. in Lavin E2). Evidence of this wide ranging intellect was clear in the earlier Broadway play, *Appearing Nitely!* (1976), where the narrator, Tess, a homeless woman, communicated with creatures from space and speculated on the nature of being.

The prominent focus in the two Broadway plays on philosophical concerns and political satire suggests the influence of Wagner. Tomlin asserts this change from her earlier comic sketches is partly due to Wagner's eclectic reading:

> She reads everything. She'll have two televisions going, two radios, 20 books, 30 magazines. Every day I'll get a stack of stuff, pages torn out of magazines with things underlined and notes in the margin, for my own edification. The range of material is mind-boggling—a discussion in a political magazine, an article in a physics publication, and a skirt at Saks (E2).

Search manifests a clear aesthetic developed over the previous sixteen years of collaboration when Tomlin and Wagner developed a confident artistic direction. An example of the forceful themes of their work, *Lily Sold Out!* (1981), performed as a television special by Tomlin, parodies art which has "sold out." By having Tomlin appear in high heels, a sequined teddy, and a top hat, it ridicules the glitzy sleaze of show business, its trademark ostentation, its mind numbing pace and indifference to character development. Tomlin sings and dances her way through "Seven Stages of Woman," including ironic numbers like "Las Vegas is My Kind of Town." In staging, with one barely clad woman and eight muscle men, *Lily Sold Out!* exposes the distorted position of women in the entertainment business, and mocks those who would pander to the lowest level of an audience's intelligence. *Search* continues in this satiric line, demanding even more from its audience and demonstrating its creators' commitment to art that is not eviscerated by commercialism. In contrast to *Lily Sold Out!*, the staging of the play *Search* (1986) uses only minimal scenic elements and Tomlin/Wagner entrust further elaboration of visual elements to the imagination of their audience. (The video of *Search* uses more elaborate scenic elements. While scenic elements were modified somewhat for the 2000 Broadway production, the show maintained its minimalistic style.) While its portrait of America is grim and chilling, it is also hopeful, pointing to humor as means of coping and connection as a means of healing the national malaise.

The undercurrent of menace and "dis-ease" in *Search* does not yield to easy solutions. Unlike the physical plague on the city of Thebes which Oedipus dispelled with a riddle, this "dis-ease" is spiritual, like the deeper corruption of Thebes which all found difficult to confront. Yet *Search*, despite the complexity of the social disorder it unearths, attempts to address the insidious influences of contemporary life, particularly as they negatively affect the lives of the characters. Reviewers have grappled with these disquieting themes and highlighted their importance. Frank Rich suggested that the play, "had illuminated that increasingly dangerous environment beyond the playhouse with a penetrating and therapeutic, if not necessarily reassuring brilliance" (196). Feminist reviewers locate the "dis-ease" more specifically: Marilyn French calls it "a world pervaded by the drive to power" (32); Lynda Hart suggests that the women characters are "caught within the sociosymbolic order dominated by the law of the Father" (2).

Characters in this troubled society walk through a world of alienation and loss where strands of emotional sustenance are frayed at best. Trudy, the play's main character, is a psychotic homeless woman who has undergone electric shock therapy and though seriously ill, still roams the streets as a castaway of Reaganomics. Most of the families are strained or split. Lud and Marie caretake their punk granddaughter, Agnus, who refers to them as "specks" and screeches out her philosophy in her act at The Unclub: "I want to insult every member of the human race."

Judith Beasley, whom we met in the Tomlin/Wagner play *Appearing Nitely!* (1976)—the anal-retentive middle-class American housewife—now sells vibrators on television: "Think of it as a kind of Hamburger Helper for the boudoir" (33). Kate, a sophisticated suburbanite, has an affair in hopes that her husband will notice. Lyn, a product of the "me" generation, divorces her New Age husband, Bob, who has fallen deeply in love with his Aikido instructor. The singles, Chrissy and Paul, fare no better.

Eaten up by fears, Chrissy cannot keep a job or find a mate; Paul, burnt out on drugs and sex, nonetheless longs for a lost child, a child whose sperm he donated one night on a fling. Ironically, Ivan, that very lost child, is the only happy child in the play, enjoying a caring and stable family life, with his two lesbian parents, Edie and Pam. The play calls out for more than coping; it calls out for healing. In this sense, Tomlin/Wagner foreground the comedian's role as licensed spokesperson and exchange the traditional role of comedian as negative exemplar for that of shaman, society's healer. By taking the shaman role further than its first emanation in their earlier one-woman show *Appearing Nitely!* (1976),

Tomlin/Wagner steer *Search* into theatrically unexplored waters. This is more than what Clive Barnes called a "confident mixture of epic seriousness and niteclub corn" (198); it is a confrontation with cultural demons.

Wagner places Trudy, the main character and narrator, in opposition to the diseased spirits and creates through her "crazy" intelligence an altered reality through which the curing ritual can take place. This positioning of Trudy reflects the positioning of the traditional shaman, somewhere between society and the spirit world. In this respect, *Search* represents a return to the roots of comedy as defined by anthropologist E. T. Kirby: "Comedy represents the antagonist in social and psychological terms, but it is a pattern based on the shaman's antagonism to diseased spirits, that which is to be driven away or eliminated" (14). Like shamanistic illusion, Wagner's play "seeks to break the surface of reality, as it were, to cause the appearance of a super-reality that is 'more real' than the ordinary" (14).

This sense of shamanistic illusion is further heightened by the transformational quality of Tomlin's performance where the characters appear and disappear as if by magic. That this form of transformational theater will make uncompromising demand on its audience is set up in Trudy's first introduction. Hunchbacked and pigeon toed, Trudy embodies the discarded, the lost, the crazy. An unlikely narrator, here is a woman whose left eye, crossed, flickers at random, and whose little mouth wads up, with unpredictable, sometimes hostile utterances:

> Look at me,
> You mammalian-brained LUNKHEADS!
> I'm not just talking to myself. I'm talking to you, too.
> And to you [pointing to members of the audience]
> and you, and you, and you and you! (13).

Trudy, a homeless Cassandra, has been doomed to tell the truth and have no one hear her. Her mind flashes in and out like a flashlight over a field on a starry night. Demanding a hearing, she guides the audience to places it did not ask to go, finally lighting corners it kept well hidden: "You people look at my shopping bags, call me crazy 'cause I save this junk. What should we call the ones who buy it?" (15) Like Crystal, the quadriplegic in *Appearing Nitely!*, Trudy gains credibility by showing no self-pity and no pretense:

> I don't want to sound negative about going crazy.
> I don't want to over romanticize it either, but frankly, goin' crazy was the best thing that ever happened to me. I don't say it's for everybody; some people couldn't cope (17).

Women's Comedy on the Stage

Once established as an empathetic character, Trudy introduces the reality shifts which pattern the whole play, literally controlling both whom the audience sees and in what order. She wanders freely into philosophical speculation: "I made some studies, and reality is the leading cause of stress amongst those in touch with it. I can take it in small doses, but as a life style I find it confining" (18). To keep up with Trudy, the listener has to leave ordinary reality and enter hers, an act that demands great speed and flexibility of thought. In addition to accompanying Trudy through her imaginative incarnations, the audience needs to know how these incarnations work, as she explains:

> It's like somebody's using my brain to dial-switch through humanity. I pick up signals that seem to transmit snatches of people's lives.
> My umbrella hat works as a satellite dish.
> I hear this sizzling white noise. Then I know it's trance time (23).

Trudy additionally challenges the audience by announcing her mission as searching out the meaning of life for her space "chums":

> We're collecting all kinds of data about life here on earth.
> We're determined to figure out, once and for all,
> just what the hell it all means (20).

To this end, Trudy interacts continuously with the audience, guiding them toward a strong performer/audience connection. The relationship Trudy establishes with the audience bears similarities to the shaman's guidance of a ritual. As Kirby points out, "Not only is the performer, the shaman, in trance and undergoing delusionary experience, but so, to a degree, is the audience" (8). As Tomlin transforms her body, the audience is asked to transform its perception. Reviewer William A. Henry III reminds us that such challenges to an audience were common in the origins of Western theater with the Greeks:

> Theater began with one actor in a mask playing all the parts, relying on his imagination and the audience's. The modern one-person show blends that ancient Greek bravado with the calculated emotional exposure of the stand-up comic. The soloist, unmasked, tells the audience what is about to take place, shaping its reactions, soliciting its affection and implying that the customers are helping create the event (201).

Rather than "customers," the audiences of *Search* are addressed as participants in a performer/writer/audience collaboration. Under the influence of the shaman, the piece calls for full audience participation so that the healing can take place.

As they toured working drafts of the script through San Diego, Seattle, Los Angeles, Portland, Austin, Lexington, Atlanta, Houston, Denver, Aspen, and

Boston before opening it in New York, Tomlin/Wagner sought audience feedback along the way. Tomlin often began the developmental show by telling the audience that it was a "work in progress," and asking for feedback. At the end of the show, an open microphone was placed in front of a camera to give Tomlin/Wagner immediate audience response (Canny). The Tomlin/Wagner intention to draw a large audience was clear from their gate charge—as little as four or five dollars. As Tomlin described it: "In Los Angeles we rented a store front, built a little stage nine inches high, hung lights and blankets and brought people in from the streets to see the show free" (qtd. in Kroll 200).

Some audience members who joined in the reality of the play claimed that it left them stunned, as if they had been in another world. Critic Frank Rich speaks of "the hallucinatory flow of consciousness as it spills about the black stage" (196). Critic Clive Barnes commented:

> Emerging into the tinsel reality of 45th Street, I soon found my bearings, and started to wonder whether this was a slight case of sleight of mind, and whether the Misses Tomlin and Wagner were as coruscating as they seemed to be at the time I was being coruscated (198).

The play, however, is not a religious ritual but a theatrical one which uses comedy not only to entertain, but to "mediate the truth," as Lawrence Mintz has suggested ("New Wave" 1). Laughter itself becomes a source of vitality as it works its way through the sobering themes of the play and strengthens the sense of community between performer and audience. As psychologist Rose Coser suggests, "The use of humor, an invitation to those who are present to join in laughter, highlights or creates group consensus" (81).

To the fractured lives of the play's characters, comedy administers a balm of the spirit. To the audience, dealing with the painful subjects of the play, comedy lends relief and perspective. These uses of humor are clear in Lyn's reflection on the failures in her family:

> Funny,
> I went into public relations because I have a way with people.
> Just not the people I'm closest to (181).

By humanizing neglected members of society, characters like Trudy, Brandy, and Tina, the play calls for greater scope and compassion in the larger society. It shows humor as egalitarian, moving easily from one group to another, one class to another, cementing connections, breaking down lies, and encouraging an attitude of survival. Comedy breaks open moments of terrifying bleakness, as in this conversation when Chrissy, an insecure working woman, describes the source of her fears:

> I'm working on overcoming my fears, Eileen,
> but it's not easy.
> At the Phobia Institute once,
> this guy in group told about a friend who was
> terrified of driving on the freeway,
> but finally she conquered her fear and got so she
> thought nothing of driving on the freeway.
> And guess what?
> She died in a freeway accident.
> That story has always stuck with me (39).

With comedy as the connecting tissue of the piece, Wagner develops a structure for the play far more complex than Tomlin's early sketch comedy. In *Search*, the character portrayals of Act I reveal many individuals who are primarily connected by coincidence, but the scope tightens in Act II to focus on three friends, intimately connected. Act II ends with Trudy giving her final reflections on her search for meaning in life. The complexity of the structure demonstrates Tomlin/Wagner's respect not only for the audience's intelligence but for their ability to handle provocative material.

Thematically the play challenges an audience to greater awareness and social responsibility by portraying a society that has abandoned children (like Agnus), pushed eccentric people (like Trudy) to the streets, and allowed government to reach barbaric levels of corruption with Watergate and Gordon Liddy. Its Act I portraits of Chrissy and Kate show a society frantically trying to feed its spiritual hunger on self-absorption. Act II portraits of Lyn, Marge, and Edie expose the Wonder Bread of the human potential movement, the emptiness of religious and ecological fads. However, the play balances this detached intellectual vision of dis-ease with Tomlin's physical passion and energy, itself offering a promise of hope, in the same way that the shaman's transformations point toward a cure. Whether it be Trudy's philosophical search, or Brandy's compassion for her Johns, or Lyn's honesty in dealing with the disappointments of her life, Tomlin's immense commitment to each character makes each worthy of respect. The performer's compassion points in the direction of cure, suggesting an alternative to the narrowly focused and self-centered lives which blind the characters.

ACT I

Act I announces the extent of the social "dis-ease" since all the characters lack connection to others, despite their sometimes desperate efforts to find it. Trudy's first trance is signaled by a lighting effect of electric current in the stage air, which clues the audience to a change in character:

> Uh Oh.
> I see this skinny punk kid.

> Got hair the color of
> Froot Loops an she's wearin' a T-shirt says
> "Leave Me Alone" (23).

When Tomlin sheds the skin of the granddaddy, Lud, and "grows into" Agnus, the granddaughter, she straightens up to full height, begins jumping on the stage and exudes the high voltage energy of a teenager. Holding an imaginary mic under new light, the audience sees Agnus, the punk kid, in her act at the Unclub:

> I'm getting my act together;
> And throwing it in your FACE.
> ... I'm Agnus Angst.
> I don't kiss ass
> I don't say thanks (84).

Abandoned and isolated, Agnus is the mega-punk rock teenager of America. While her mother works as a performance artist in Europe, Agnus spends her time destroying every connection to family and friend she has left. "I look at my family. I feel like a detached retina" (88). She spits in her gene-splicing father's petri dish and yells at her grandparents as she goes out the door: "DON'T WAIT UP" (82). She rankles under middle class clichés of her grandfather, "You'd better learn some manners, young lady, or ... people won't like you," and abuses her audience (79).

Agnus is one of the most important characters in the play because she tells a young person's truth about the American culture. In Tomlin's energetic portrayal, Agnus' pain is palpable, her disconnection screaming out from each pore. With fierce intelligence she confronts an older generation that has left her without models and without hope. Agnus shows signs of intelligent life in her ability to list the disappointments of her generation, born after Viet Nam when charlatans received the attention of celebrities and celebrities overdosed themselves to death. In her act, Agnus chants out her retort to the national degeneration, the failure of ideals. Her attempts at numbness are the spiritual equivalent of body-piercing, a soul-piercing to harden her pain:

> And I don't mind it
> when I first came into
> this world
> Elvis was already fat.
>
> I don't mind
> I was born
> at the time of the crime
> known as Watergate

> And must've missed out on most things
> that made America great. But I don't mind it.
>
> I don't mind
> each morning when I get up
> I feel like I want to vomit.
> I don't mind that
> the teenage suicide rate
> is soaring like Haley's comet (98).

At the end of her act, having taken as her guru G. Gordon Liddy, the Watergate break-in mastermind, Agnus holds her hand over a burning candle in order to inure herself to pain. By the end of the second act, she has thrown away her latchkey and is roaming the streets. Brandy and Tina, the prostitutes, mark her for "the life," but not for survival.

Despite her pain and her capacity for self-destruction, Agnus is funny. What is the basis of this humor? How does her character further inform us about the Tomlin/Wagner humor? What would crush a normal teenager makes Agnus furious, and her abuse of anyone within reach strikes like a huge wave crashing on a cold shore. That indomitable spirit contributes to her humor, because as she registers each repulsion in her muscle system, her passionate responses have the humor of predictability. Agnus warrants attention because her self-righteous indignation has substance to it. Through her confrontations with adults, Agnus confronts a troubled society with a vitriol that is at once entertaining and informative. In dealing with the painful break-up of a family, Wagner writes scenes leavened by humor, as when Agnus' grandfather tries to translate his granddaughter's punk appearance to the neighbor down the street:

> Old man Sanders stopped me today; says he
> saw somethin' odd lookin' in the yard—says it was downright eerie!
> Worried we might have poltergeists (81).

Tomlin plays both characters as if they are on a couch, turning one way and the other. Her country accent is slow as Lud ponders this matter of a strange and alienated grandchild:

> I had to say, "No that wasn't no poltergeist,
> that was my granddaughter.
> She glows in the dark cause her necklace is a
> reflective flea collar."
> How do you think that makes me feel? (81).

In addition to their disconnection from Agnus, the grandparents have their own tensions. Lud assumes dominance over Marie and casually insults her with lines like:

> You've got a brain like a hummingbird...
> Makes you appear dense and at the same time flighty.
> If I couldn't think of who it was said somethin' ...
> I'd simply keep my mouth shut. Somethin' I wish you'd consider more often.
>
> MARIE
> I used to tolerate that kind of talk, because I told myself your hernia made you so hateful.
> I have let you walk all over me.
> Janet used to beg me, she'd say, "Mama, please join a consciousness-raising group" (67).

This simple country couple struggles together to bring their granddaughter back to her former self. The night of Agnus' Unclub act Granddaddy and Grandma Speck wait up for Agnus and plan to greet her wearing little milk mustaches, like they did when she was a little girl. But the girl never comes home. On the street, she catches the eye of Tina and Brandy, two prostitutes:

> What's she call us, Tina? Some kind of "speck"?
> That baby brat ain't in the life—not yet.
> She's just another runaway. But in a few weeks,
> she'll be all different... Ever see a stray dog
> on the streets? I can tell just like that
> which ones will survive and which one won't. I don't know how I can
> tell but I can tell (121).

In their own world of disconnection on the streets, Brandy and Tina use humor to survive. Speaking of a stray dog, Brandy says, "She just never kicked into the survival mode like you need to—to survive, like you and me did, Tina" (125). Gum cracking, wary of some strangers, full of colorful speech, they are two of Tomlin's most vital characters. To become them, Tomlin sits in one place and turns in one direction and then another. Like Trudy, they have a particular confidence and acceptance of their usefulness. They have a pride in what they do, because they see their work as helping people survive:

> BRANDY
> I could be a shrink. I should hang out a shingle.
> People tell me things. Forget it. Things they
> don't even tell people they're close to . . .
> I swear people don't want sex so much as they want somebody
> who'll listen to 'em . . .

TINA
Yeah, that's the first thing you learn after fellatio is how to listen (126).

Humor further exposes the truth of vacuous misspent lives in the portraits of Chrissy and Kate. In contrast to the castaway lives of Trudy and Agnus, Chrissy and Kate are self-indulgent women who create many of their own problems, but keep themselves blind to the problems of others. Tomlin first shows Chrissy doing strenuous aerobics in a gym. Between very fast breaths, Chrissy talks to her friend, Eileen, about her inability to hold down a job:

> It's not that I lack ambition. I am ambitious in the sense that I want to
> be more than I am now. But if I were truly ambitious, I think I'd
> already be more than I am now. A sobering thought, Eileen.
> What if, right at this very moment,
> I AM living up to my full potential? (35, 37).

Almost all her sentences begin with "I"; every action we see her perform concerns her personal beauty, as we see Tomlin mime showering, putting on panty-hose, heels, clothes, applying make-up, and fluffing her hair. Since all events are judged only in so far as they impact her directly, Chrissy speaks in a breathy, hurried voice. All emotional matters are made serious with a whisper:

> Once... I've been wanting to tell someone this, Eileen... once I came
> this close to committing suicide (43).

Equally self-absorbed, Kate waits impatiently for Bucchi, her hairdresser, to fix her hair cut, since to her great alarm, one side is very short and the other long. In her portrayal of Kate, Tomlin has a very straight back, and pages carelessly through *Town and Country* magazine. She has a throaty, breathy voice, which drags out the syllables, and over-enunciates her consonants, as in saying her friend's name, "Lon-nie." Everything Kate says is coated in cynicism; her face is this side of a sneer, and she can't work up enthusiasm for anything in her life:

> I tell you, coming here today was so humiliating.
> There were people in the streets actually staring at my haircut.
> People who normally would be intimidated....
> Lonnie, you must read this article I've just finished. Fascinating. It's
> all about how you can actually die from boredom. Yes. "A slow
> agonizing death." They've done studies (53).

These portraits present another harsh view of the age; they sit as scathing indictments of a class system without compassion and a human potential movement which crippled its adherents. At the same time, as humor exposes truth in the lives of Kate and Chrissy, it helps the characters cope. These initial sketches of women in Act I prepare for more extended character portraits of Act II, where a group of three women friends contend with personal and political turmoil.

ACT II

At first the "dis-ease" of Act I appears to be answered by the characters in Act II who have "found" the women's movement. However, as lives of the Act II characters unfold, their losses appear to be as great as characters in Act I, and their disappointment greater, since they have put their trust in a movement or in institutions that did not satisfy their need for connection. This "radical critique of the status quo" led critic Frank Rich to call Act II "the most genuinely subversive comedy to be produced on Broadway in years" (196).

Lyn, the central character of Act II, committed to women's liberation, steers a rocky course between family, job, friends, and her political beliefs, concluding that "it's hard to be politically conscious and upwardly mobile at the same time" (193). A rare analysis of the personal effect of the women's movement on the lives of individuals, the sketch is sometimes harsh, finding that even the smallest amount of political change comes at a high price in the lives of individuals.

The piece begins and ends at a garage sale outside Lyn's geodesic dome, where she discovers her autographed copy of the first issue of *Ms.* magazine, signed by Gloria Steinem. Literally, the events of Lyn and her two friends, Marge and Edie, are framed between the historical moments of the Women's March For Equality in 1970 and the nomination speech of Geraldine Ferraro for Vice President, nominee of the Democratic Party in 1984. It contrasts the effects of liberation on women of three different lifestyles: Edie, the radical lesbian; Marge, a single woman with an alcohol problem; and Lyn, their friend, wife, mother, working woman, the central character of the sketch.

In Act II Tomlin's transformations become more intense as characters move in and out of her body very quickly. The "fevered script" (Watts 192) demands absolute audience attention as Tomlin demonstrates her virtuosity as a shape changer, instantaneously shedding one character to embody another. A many-sided conversation may have only a few lines for each character. In this interchange, for example, three friends inject each other with the truth serum of comedy:

> MARGE [to Edie]
> I mean, honey, you couldn't be more antiwar,
> but if it weren't for army surplus you'd have nothing to wear.
> Lyn, I'm not exaggerating. Edie was in my plant store yesterday in
> those camouflage overalls.
> I almost watered her.

EDIE
Oh, Marge has taste in everything, except when it comes to men.
Marge, the "Lib" in women's Lib stands for liberation, not libido.
I mean, what good is it, Sis, to have sexual freedom if you become a slave to it? You've got Cosmo damage. . . . and who says we need to shave under our arms? Ta-Dah!
LYN
Body hair! A sure way to tell the radicals from the "middle-of-the roaders," like me. . . . Edie, you're probably on some FBI list of the politically most dangerous (145–6).

In the following fast paced scene, Tomlin reveals Marge's steady movement toward alcoholism. An important scene, it prepares the audience for Marge's eventual death by suicide, a consequence of rape and desertion by her lover. Tomlin totally changes voice and body to inhabit the speaking character. The performer lowers her voice and changes her stance as she becomes Edie, the toughest of the trio, the most political. To play Marge, Tomlin stretches her spine and raises her head to suggest Marge's superiority and worldliness. Lyn is heterosexual, naive, the well-intentioned peace maker whose voice is pure and whose stance is balanced:

MARGE [low, cynical]
Hell, my whole life feels like one big isolation tank. Okay, please, don't go to any trouble, you two; I'll pour my own drink.
LYN [kindly]
Marge, it's so ironic. I mean that a woman as nurturant as you could be so self-destructive.
MARGE [overly casual]
I'll tell you what's ironic... The rapist made off with my Mark Cross rape whistle.
BOB
I'm glad to see you looking so good.
LYN
The bruises are all gone (171).

As the play intensifies, so does the integration between body and emotion. As Tomlin's transformations become more fast-paced, the themes become more serious. As Jack Kroll suggests "what seems like a gag situation explodes into something deeper and more moving" (200). When Marge does commit suicide, the curve of Tomlin's back, the slump of her head, tell us that this is a very serious loss to Lyn:

Oh, Bob, something terrible.
Marge is dead!
She's hanged herself (187).

Even at this tragic time, though, humor enters the scene as Lyn determines to hold her home together. After Marge's funeral Lyn, heartfully, turns in bed to Bob:

> I will be Mega-Mom,
> Wonder
> Working
> Woman
> Willing Wife.
> I will even be the Total Woman...
> at least for a night or two.
> I don't want us to lose what we have.
> [snoring] Bob? Bob? (*Search* video).

The Tomlin/Wagner humor carries serious weight, pushed to the limit to even moderately balance the degree of sadness exposed in the lives of the characters. Howard Kissel comments on the Tomlin/Wagner ability to show the "odd beauty as well as the comedy in their poignant lives" (198). Rather than mitigate pain, humor here lends courage, a stance the poet Yeats describes as "open eyed and laughing" (283). The writing injects humor even when Lyn expresses anger. Here she confronts her husband, Bob, for imposing his values on her:

> Bob, you expect too much of me.
> It's one thing to be a modern housewife, career woman, mother. . . .
> No, I have to be organic, holistic, learn millet recipes, grow wheat grass,
> make beet juice, wait around for sourdough to rise.
> Well, it just so happens the last sourdough . . . was
> Play-Doh (185).

As a way of examining the failures of the women's movement, Lyn's life reads like a video on fast-forward. To answer the demands of her husband or the buzzer of her boss, Tomlin as Lyn keeps a frantic pace, rushing from one side of the stage to another. Ignoring Lyn's children, her boss, Sindell, schedules her for weekend conferences targeting "Women on the Way Up," to learn about power dressing. Finally, when she does not receive a promotion, Lyn confronts her boss, and reports to her husband: "I wanted to take the scarf-ruffle-tie thing from around my neck and strangle him" (189). Wagner's words and Tomlin's frenzied enactment question the "advances" in women's lives brought about by the "freedom" to overwork.

Humor and pain mingle again in the scenes regarding Lyn's two small children. Pushed by her husband to be more nurturing, her boss to be more efficient, and her friends to be more radical, Lyn loses control of her children, as this conversation with their teacher indicates:

> I had no idea they'd taken the bats to school with
> them. Believe me, it will not happen again.
> Look, just give a list of the damage and I will
> pay for it. I'm sorry, I'm raising two
> Darth Vaders (186).

An imaginative sound design suggests the presence of the children screaming in the yard. It brings the other characters on stage appropriately and maintains the emotional pressure on Lyn, where, for example, the audience hears the imperious tones of the boss' buzzer commanding Lyn into his office or the audience hears the onions hitting the chopping board when she fights with her husband.

Lyn also uses humor to pursue the truth. It accompanies her as a friend when she needs its bravado to get to the bottom of her feelings, as in this confrontation with Bob when she has found out he is having an affair:

> Who is she? Some horny herbalist?
> Is it that checkout girl at the Health-Mart?
> ... She probably has time to make good money and to meditate.
> Don't tell me her tofu tastes like lasagna. ... Feel free to interrupt
> me at anytime (190).

In this same vein, Lyn shoots back this response to the psychiatrist when he suggests that her troubles are due to premenstrual syndrome:

> Premenstrual syndrome?
> I mean, I'm getting divorced. I'm raising twin boys.
> I have a lot of job pressure—I've got to find one.
> The ERA didn't pass, not long ago I lost a very dear friend,
> and...and my husband is involved...
> not just involved, but in love, I'm afraid...with this woman...
> who's quite a bit younger than I am.
> And you think it's my period and not my life? (191)

Marge and Lyn's unhappy lives suggest not just poor choices but failure in the overriding belief system to which they have subscribed. Marge's willingness to give herself away to her lovers and Lyn's loss of self between the demands of work and home have resulted in suicide for the former and divorce for the latter. Humor leavens the pain, but humor is not the end of these sketches as one observer from the development show in Austin observed in a letter to Tomlin: "As I watched you, I wondered how deeply you have had to immerse yourself in the pain you are naming for us, to be able to hog-tie it with humor and present it to us using a form that we can bear to see" (qtd. in Kroll 200).

Wagner's script proposes that women's friendship can be an alternative to despair, and highlights occur as the women laugh together. When Edie visits Lyn to tell her the sad news that she and Pam and their child, Ivan, are moving to New York for Ivan's music, Edie interjects:

> Yeah! Ivan's gonna' play a solo with that Suzuki group of kids at Carnegie Hall. Can you believe that turkey-baster kid's a prodigy? I knew we had something special when he was born on Thanksgiving (192).

In the final moments of the Lyn sketch, Lyn calls Edie in New York to share her exhilaration when the first female Vice Presidential candidate took to the floor of the Democratic Convention:

> I called Edie tonight during the nomination.
> We stayed on the phone together.
> When we heard, "Ladies and gentlemen of the
> convention, my name is Geraldine Ferraro,"
> we cried. Earlier when the newscaster
> on ABC had said,
> "She kept her maiden name,
> not for any feminist reason,
> but because she feels she owes
> her mother so much,"
> we laughed (194).

This section of the play shows in microcosm what the whole play is trying to do with humor: expand its use, show its depth, let it reveal character. Not only does humor tighten pain, but it also explores it. In this play, humor is itself a probe, exploring areas of culture, formerly mythologized, possibly aggrandized. Two avowed feminists, Tomlin and Wagner reject a superficial assessment of the Women's Movement and prefer to look at it with some distance, a distance which lights up some of its failures. At the same time, the play encourages a clear-headed acceptance of the reality of this era, a remarkable era when many women sacrificed to extend personal and political freedom to women. But in keeping with the Tomlin/Wagner aesthetic, the play offers no easy answers to the difficult role of being a whole person in a fractured society.

In the final section of Act II, when Trudy reappears to report her findings on her mission for her space chums to discover the meaning of life, the play moves from concerns of the individual to those of the metaphysical. Beyond its placement of hope in individual characters, the play celebrates the transcendence found in laughing together, in the communal art of theater, and in the interconnection of common experience. At the end of the play, Kate, a rich suburbanite, recalls a moment for her of rare communication:

> This evening after the concert, I saw these two prostitutes on the corner...talking with this street crazy, this bag lady. And I actually stopped to watch them.

> Even though it had begun to rain. . . . I saw this young man go up, obviously from out of town, and he asked them, "How do I get to Carnegie Hall?" And the bag lady said, "Practice!" And we caught each other's eyes—the prostitutes, the bag lady, the young man and I. We all burst out laughing. There we were, laughing together, in the pouring rain, and then the bag lady did the dearest thing—she offered me her umbrella hat. She said that I needed it more than she did, because one side of my hair was beginning to shrink. And, Lonnie, I did the strangest thing. I took it! (210).

By reaching outside her closed world, Kate begins to get some perspective on the extent of her selfishness. In this sense, Kate stands for those individuals who have a failure of caring, but who have the possibility of change. This last section of the play focuses on what critic Linda Winer describes as Tomlin and Wagner's concerns about "seeking and caring, and the mystery—if not the meaning—of life" (199). In opposition to the prison of the individual, the play places a high value on communal experience, summarized by the "goosebump experience." At the end of the play Trudy takes her space chums to Lily's play. But they don't watch the performer, they watch the audience:

> **TRUDY**
> We were at the back of the theater, standing there in the dark, all of a sudden I feel one of 'em tug my sleeve, whispers, "Trudy, look." "Yeah, goose bumps. You definitely got goose bumps. You really like the end of the play that much?" They said it wasn't the play; it was the audience.... Yeah, to see strangers sitting together in the dark, laughing and crying about the same things...that just knocked 'em out (212).

Trudy suggests that the human importance of a play is the connection of performer and audience, the emotional effect of the performer on the audience. Whereas the hierarchy of performer over audience disrupts connection, the communication between the two creates it.

Returning, then, to the question posed at the beginning of this chapter, "What would comedy by women look like if it were culturally unrestricted?," we have, I propose, a play that we may use as an answer. Tomlin/Wagner's bold choices have potentially moved the center for comedians further toward political and social commentary. Common now in performance is the link between feminist values and comedy, between an intelligent viewpoint and comedy, between the painful truth and comic entertainment. On the human scale, Wagner's play asserts values of connection over competition, of egalitarianism over domination, and of hope over despair (French 34). In respectfully portraying lives of women, many of them misfits struggling against obstacles in their lives, Wagner emphasizes their common humanity and widens their appeal. Though the ending of the play has been criticized as sentimental (Rich 147), the play's ending does not disrupt the dominant tone of the whole. By insisting upon truthful portrayal of their characters, but never avoiding painful subjects, Tomlin and Wagner deviate from popular entertainment's tendency towards escapism or easy ridicule and they invite their audience to follow.

Search is a critique of the American culture: its over-readiness to settle for the easy answer, to go with the trend, its refusal to cope with painful reality. Yet the Tomlin/Wagner comedy encourages laughter at foibles and most especially at systemic evil. The unrelenting intelligence of the work exposes the failure of systems: greed in corporations, corruption of power in government, self-centeredness in families, and rigidity in gender systems. Their characters show the human results of systems that cannot act compassionately. Against the failure of these institutions, they pose the spirit of the individual and the power of community. A review in *Variety* of the 2000 production in New York commented on the play's call for community: "This exceptional piece of theatre is a salutary reminder that a civilization's health may best be measured not by the cumulative wealth of its citizens but by the community of feeling that binds them together." Discarded as useless by the official culture, characters like Trudy are aflame with vitality, demonstrating a national waste, a national joke.

To the lengthening tradition of women and solo performance, Jane Wagner and Lily Tomlin added substance and weight. Their contribution of *Search* stands as a high point in the movement of women's solo performance. If Diller began by cracking open the door of women's comedy and wedging herself into the room, Tomlin/Wagner proudly occupy the room. They have not only rearranged the furniture, they have remodeled it to suit a woman's viewpoint. While Diller essentially used the traditional standup joke form and content, highlighting the absurdity of the idealization of women, Tomlin/Wagner break further into the theatrical form of the one-woman show and particularly emphasize their role as licensed spokespersons.

The depth and substance of the work of Jane Wagner and Lily Tomlin form a solid base from which female comedians like Kate Clinton and Paula Poundstone can occupy the stage. Women with one-woman shows like Gilda Radner and Whoopi Goldberg had a beacon to guide them in the work of Lily Tomlin and Jane Wagner. Although Jane Wagner and Lily Tomlin could not build their own work on brilliant models, because few existed, they could pass on the high standard they developed to young female comedians like Margaret Cho and Ellen DeGeneres. With the addition of their work, what seemed impossible in Diller's day, contentious in Roseanne's, was becoming not only acceptable but in demand.

Chapter Six

Feminist Humor and Change
The Works of Kate Clinton, Paula Poundstone, and Whoopi Goldberg

> Consider feminist humor and consider the lichen. Growing low and lowly on enormous rock, secreting tiny amounts of acid, year after year, eating into the rock. Making places for water to gather, to freeze and crack the rock a bit. Making soil, making way for grasses to grow. Making way for rosehips and sea oats, for aspen and cedar. It is the lichen which begins the splitting apart of the rocks, the changing of the shoreline, the shape of the earth. Feminist humor is serious, and it is about the changing of this world.[1]
>
> Kate Clinton, "Making Light: Some Notes on Feminist Humor"

A HALF CENTURY OF WOMEN'S SOLO PERFORMANCE COMEDY REVEALS significant changes, a progression marked by the contrast between Diller's description of her entertainment as "pure fun," and Kate Clinton's description of her contemporary stand-up as "serious." Clinton's phrase, the "changing of the shoreline," becomes visible in the work of Lily Tomlin and Jane Wagner, feminists whose comedy envisions a culture which equally values men and women, a culture which Tomlin observed is far from the current one: "The entire culture is built as a support system for men and men's values. One of those values is that women are providers and accommodate to the system. We really should be developing a system that values men and women equally" (qtd. in Judge 16). Likewise, Roseanne turned the persona she had developed in her stand-up into one of the most influential television personalities of the '80s and '90s. She felt that her show *Roseanne!* was primarily about changing women's lives: "I intended to change the way women thought of themselves, and our children and our relationships. I had great passion for this message. I feel like I was the woman for the times. I got to be a woman who carries that torch" (qtd. in Mansfield 6).

Motivating these superstars of comedy and many contemporary feminist stand-ups has been a desire to continually reduce restrictions on women's lives. Contemporary stand-ups Kate Clinton and Paula Poundstone use their stand-up to help move society forward on the equity scale. Actress and comedian Whoopi

Goldberg has committed much of her life's work to issues of gender and race equity. Margaret Cho mocks the standard of beauty expected of women in much of her routine. Ellen DeGeneres used her prominence to work for more tolerance toward gays. These women demonstrate that women's comedy has its edge precisely because it is not man's comedy. Much of its substance comes from its point of view.

WOMEN'S VERSION OF TRUTH

A defining characteristic of feminist solo comedy is its positing of women's truth and experience to replace the myths of the patriarchy. Having traced this point of view from Diller's work through Roseanne's, I would now like to delineate some of its salient characteristics in the work of feminist comedians who have worked in the 1980s, '90s, and 2000s. Although I will touch upon this theme in the works of contemporary stand-ups, Kate Clinton, Paula Pounsdstone, and Whoopi Goldberg, it is significant that a feminist viewpoint informs the work of a growing number of women stand-up performers. The stand-up work that women like Margaret Cho and Ellen DeGeneres do shows strong influence of a feminist viewpoint.

The work of feminist theorist Elin Diamond provides a background for a discussion of this thrust in women's solo performance comedy. Diamond argues that the issue of "truth" in Western civilization has been particularly exclusive of women's reality. For feminists this "truth"—usually understood as Truth, a neutral, omnipotent, changeless essence—is inseparable from gender-based and biased epistemologies.... In all cases, the epistemological, morphological, *universal* standard for measuring the true is the masculine, the universal male that stands for God the Father (363-4). Diamond contends that feminists cannot, however, simply dismiss truth and banish it as a patriarchal trapping.

> But feminism, whose empirical, historical project continues to be the recovery of women's texts and activities, has a stake in truth—in contributing to the accumulation and organization of knowledge by which a culture values or forgets its past, attends to the divergences of the present (364).

Feminist stand-up heightens this "stake in truth" because it specializes in revealing hidden truths. The assertion of counter-truths and counter-experiences has been key to contemporary women's feminist stand-up. Characteristic of this movement are: 1) the presentation of the woman's body in ways that diverge from mainstream cultural expectations; 2) the foregrounding of woman's experience; and 3) the use of personal experience and observation to serve a political end.

THE WOMAN'S BODY IN FEMINIST STAND-UP

In the contemporary feminist stand-up that I have viewed, the body of the woman performer is there not as a theatrical sign for "the male gaze," but as a theatrical sign representing woman as performer with something to say, Mintz's "licensed spokesperson" role. This represents a significant shift in the identity of a woman performer in relation to an audience. As Sue Ellen Case explains, "In the realm of audience reception, the gaze is encoded with culturally determined components of male sexual desire, perceiving 'woman' as sexual object" (118). As film critic E. Ann Kaplan asserts, "the male gaze" privileges the male viewpoint. In opposition to this, feminist stand-up privileges the feminist viewpoint. Therefore, it is common, for example, for a feminist comedian to dress to suit herself, with indifference toward her sexual allure. This relative freedom has evolved from a history of confrontation with the issue. I have argued that Diller's costuming was a necessary block to the "male gaze," which she felt could have derailed her performance (Diller, Interview). Her development of the "negative exemplar" role served multiple purposes, but one was to reverse the expectations of "the male gaze," from one of a woman's body seen as a sexual object to one of performer's body seen as a source of humor. Likewise, Roseanne deflected "the male gaze" by making jokes about being fat and challenging the assumptions of a beauty standard based on thinness. By understating her dress of simple pants and a top, Paula Poundstone drew little attention to her body in the performances I saw in 1995 and 1996. This "non-costume" served practical purposes, giving Poundstone the freedom to walk around the stage, roll on the floor, and jump off the stage to interchange with audience members.

Even so, the presentation of her body for a feminist stand-up remains an issue open to continuous negotiation with cultural concerns and the immediate audience. One stand-up I saw in 1994 in a midnight show in Aspen didn't even try to talk down hecklers or deal with drunk rude remarks; instead, she began her show by quickly taking off her shirt and doing her act in her bra. There was a sense that she wanted to confront the body issue, just so she could move on to her comedy act. Sandra Bernhard also confronted hecklers in a 2003 Denver performance. Several times during the basement club performance men yelled out remarks about her body. She ignored the first man and lambasted the second. When she left the stage after the show, she came out for the encore in her bra. This action had a completely different sense from that of the Aspen comic. There was no sense of accommodating the hecklers, but rather a sense that she was in charge of her own body and what she did with it. It was as if Bernhard was saying, "So what, let's just celebrate a good time." As one of the comedians in the film *Wisecracks* said, "They'll look at you twice. Once to see your tits, the other to see what you're doing."

WOMEN'S EXPERIENCE

Feminist stand-up foregrounds women's experiences and perceptions. In stand-up a woman becomes the subject and center of the performance, even though her content may appeal to men and women. This shift of woman performer as subject rather than object represents a historical advance for women in performance. In this sense, feminist stand-up resists the dominance of "the male gaze," one of the major obstacles to women's performance. As Sue Ellen Case asserts, "For women one of the results of this representation of woman as 'Other' in the male gaze is that she also becomes 'Other' to herself. Within the patriarchal system of signs, women do not have the cultural mechanisms of meaning to construct themselves as the subject rather than as the object of performance" (120). Successful negotiation of the stand-up form and unique audience/performer relationship provide a performer with what Case calls the "mechanics of meaning to construct [herself] as subject" (120).

Breaking then from the patriarchal system of signs, the feminist stand-up foregrounds herself as subject and speaks her version of truth. There is a sense among many contemporary stand-ups that women's shared experience will unite the audience, even though the audience is commonly made up of men and women. As I demonstrated earlier, Roseanne's stand-up centered on women's shared experience and viewpoint, and often her routines positioned men as listeners to conversations among women. One of Roseanne's strengths, however, was to somehow elicit the empathy of men, even though they were not always the subjects and were often the targets of her jokes.

THE PERSONAL/POLITICAL

The personal becomes political in feminist comedy because a feminist comic intends to confront the oppression of women. As a result, her stories or jokes carry with them a meaning beyond their literal one-liner laugh weight. For example, when contemporary comedian, Liz Winstead says, "I think, therefore I'm single" (qtd. in Barreca *Penguin* 612), the joke has several levels of humor. The joke has several levels of humor. The economy of the joke is funny in itself as a parody of Descartes. But more than that, the joke challenges a world-view. If male rationality is the crowning glory of the phallocentric world-view, then a woman who remains single or not united with a man can escape the limits of phallocentricism and create her own world of meaning.

By foregrounding her own experience and reality, the feminist stand-up works to dismantle patriarchal norms and notions. In this sense, the movement from the more formal joke set of traditional stand-up to the informal personal reflection or story becomes very important. A contrast between the formal farcical joke pattern of Phyllis Diller and the informal story pattern of contemporary stand-up, Carrie Snow, illustrates this point. The following segment from the

Feminist Humor and Change

opening of Phyllis Diller's 1996 Lake Tahoe performance represents the traditional comic's dependence on highly exaggerated reality or farce. Diller's joke inventions center on the life of a woman who does not exist, one created for "pure fun." To foreground her intent to entertain, Diller appears in a wildly colored striped sequin dress, a huge blond wig, gold lamé boots, and long gold gloves:

> You think I'm overdressed. This is my slip. Now I'm going to tell you the truth about what I'm wearing. I used to work as a lampshade in a whorehouse. I couldn't get one of the good jobs. You see I never grew tits. They're in there. God knows, I tried. I did that exercise where you press your hands together and make your bust larger. My hands got bigger. I wear so damn much rubber, no matter which way I fall I leave skid marks. When they fit me for a bra, they use a level. My friend told me to stuff my bra with Kleenex. I wish to hell she had told me to take them out of the box. For two weeks I had square boobs.

By contrast, Carrie Snow uses material that she presents as her own experience:

> I had a second date and I'm pretty proud of myself. I have rules now. Things that you shouldn't do so you can get to a second date. I've had a lot of first dates. Yeah, if you go out on a first date, never take off your shoe and pick up objects with your feet. Guys get so scared when you do monkey shit. I had a second date and we were having tea, and we were putting honey in our tea, and I said, "You know, honey is just bee vomit." [Comic laughs] And I never saw him again either (qtd. in *Wisecracks*).

Far different from Diller's inventions, Snow's story exposes some of the actual constraints dating imposes on ordinary women. Snow implicitly ridicules the concessions women make to succeed in the dating arena, and she further suggests that dating privileges men more than women. As I have argued earlier, Diller's humor is formal, memorized, and controlled, whereas the contemporary feminist stand-up is more personal, apparently less memorized, and apparently less controlled, since the comedian will often stop mid-sentence and spontaneously interchange with the audience. Diller derives laughter from the lack of reality, the impossibility of her situations. An evolution in feminist comedy is its use of more personal material that widens the goal of feminist comedy to include social change as well as entertainment.

Robin Tyler, a contemporary stand-up, underscores the importance of the connection between the speaker and her experience:

> So now you have a woman there with a mic, that you have to listen to. She is not a ballet dancer being caught by a man. She is not an opera singer, waiting for the man to get home. She is not a blues singer saying that though her man has beat her...she loves him so. All of a sudden there's a woman there

> with a microphone that's saying, "Hey, excuse me, this is what happened to me. This is what I feel, this is how I'm telling it" (qtd. in *Wisecracks*).

Anne Beatts, a contemporary comedy writer, affirms the importance of a strong personal point of view in comedy: "Behind my desire to shock is an even stronger desire to evade the 'feminine' stereotype: 'You say women are afraid of mice? I'll show you! I'll eat the mouse!'" Beatts says that since she knows what her position is and what the issues are, she has no trouble pinpointing her humor: "Obviously, it's wrong for the woman in the ring-around-the-collar commercials to be foundering in the depths of misery because her husband has a ring around his collar. Why doesn't he wash his own damn shirt?" (qtd. in Barreca, *Penguin* 59–60).

In line with Beatts' vision of feminist comedy, some women stand-ups claim that they became professional stand-ups in order to communicate their reality, their version of truth. Emily Levine tells how she became discouraged when the reality of men's experience always took precedence over her own experience:

> I started with an all-male comedy group, except for me. It was an improv group, and I was always the girl. The men were astronauts, the men were cowboys, the men were businessmen, the men were troubadours, and I was always the girl. I didn't know how to compete in that context. Men think their version of reality is reality. I like my version of reality to be the dominant one (qtd. in *Wisecracks*).

One of the most important contributions of women's feminist stand-up is the voice it gives to funny women who do not easily fit into the mainstream. Kate Clinton, a comedian with a sharp political insight, and Paula Poundstone, a single mother and political commentator, have views too strong to be considered "ready for prime time." (Poundstone's attempt at an ABC prime-time slot lasted two episodes (Dumas 9D)). Nonetheless, both of them have continued to perform in the comedy circuits and their roles as political commentators are widely recognized. In addition, the work of actor/comedian Whoopi Goldberg has focused on issues of poverty, race, and women to highlight areas of social and economic inequity.

KATE CLINTON: POLITICAL ACTIVISM ON THE "LESCOM" CIRCUIT

Intelligent, creative, and articulate, Kate Clinton's is one of the most sophisticated comedians of our time. A feminist committed to social change, she is also one of the most revolutionary. Born in 1947 in Buffalo, N.Y., she drew her first laughs entertaining her large Catholic family. She attended LeMoyne College, a Jesuit school, in Syracuse, N.Y., where even in those pre-feminist times she felt the absence of women in the curriculum, and she went on to teach high school English for eight years. Her wake-up call came when she studied for a year at the Women Writer's Center, outside of Syracuse. She was inspired and changed by the work of many women writers. In her book, *Don't Get Me Started*, she tells of reading the works of Susan Glaspell, Kate Chopin, Zora Neale Hurston, and Mary Daly and of hearing visiting writers including Rita Mae Brown, Marge Piercy, and Adrienne Rich read from their works. Adrienne Rich encouraged Clinton to write about women and humor and Clinton consequently formulated her ideas in an essay, "Making Light" (9–11). Wrestling with a philosophical basis for comedy helped Clinton build a stand-up career marked by confidence, clarity, and a sense of mission.

Clinton's partner of many years, Urvashi Vaid, is also committed to activism for a more socially equitable society. Vaid was named by *Time* magazine as one of the fifty young leaders to watch in the new century and by *A. Magazine* as one of the twenty-five most influential Asian Americans. She was the executive director of the Gay and Lesbian Task Force for three years and has been credited with making gay and lesbian issues more prominent. A lawyer as well as an activist, Vaid has worked for the ACLU, addressing such issues as prison conditions, and other concerns of importance to disenfranchised Americans. Her book, *Virtual Equality*, criticizes the mainstreaming of gays as ultimately injurious to their rights.[2]

Clinton began her long career as a comedian in 1981, when a friend booked her a club date. Performing at first in small coffee shops and clubs, her strong following led her to do national concert tours. In her book, *Don't Get Me Started*, she says she started writing about lesbians because "What's funniest is what is truest and I was interested in telling the truth about my life" (13). She has been inspired since the beginning of her career by a quote from the poet, Muriel Rukeyser, "When a woman tells the truth of her life, the world splits open" (13). Clinton's career line corresponds to the growth of the Women's Movement. Her comedy has always been essentially feminist in its concerns with the empowerment of women, and her primary audience has been lesbians. In her concert *Read These Lips* she jokes about gender inequities in the contraceptive battle. She makes light of the fact that it took twelve years to legalize the contraceptive for women, RU486, and overnight to approve Viagra for men: "Does Bob like it? Let the dance begin! Bob Dole took Viagra and his arm went up."

Clinton's comedy has also steadily grown more political and more socially satiric. *Don't Get Me Started* tells how her comedy was radicalized when she was one of the emcees of the March on Washington in 1987. As she passed the AIDS Quilt laid out at dawn of that morning, she saw gathered around the quilt many people connected to the lost lives represented there, and she realized then that her comedy had to include more serious subjects. She believes in the power of laughing and crying at the same time (14–15). About her growing reputation as an insightful political comedian, Clinton told an interviewer for *Womankind* that she feels more able to do political comedy now that there are many more lesbian comedians.

Clinton's reputation as a political analyst and comedian has been strengthened by her commentary for CNN and MSNBC, her appearances on many talk shows such as *Good Morning America*, *Nightline*, and *The Roseanne Show*, and her hosting the gay and lesbian show *In the Life*. She wrote for *The Rosie O'Donnell Show* during its first six months, and her columns appear monthly in *The Progressive* and *The Advocate*. In addition, she has written for *The New York Times* and *George* magazine. Her book, *Don't Get Me Started*, was published in 1998 by Ballantine, and Publisher's Weekly named its taped version "One of 1998's Best Audiobooks."[3]

Clinton's performance career has met with popular success both on the road and in theatres. She has six comedy albums, including *Read These Lips*, *Comedy You Can Dance To*, and *Babes in Joyland*. Her 2000 tour, *Y2K8*, opened at the Public Theatre in New York. *Correct Me if I'm Right*, her 1999 show, opened off-Broadway at the Westbeth Theatre Center, while her 1993 show, *Out Is In*, had a three-month Off-Broadway run after it played in Los Angeles. In New York during December 2001 and January 2002, Clinton acted in the production of *The Vagina Monologues*.

CLINTON'S PERFORMANCE

Clinton cuts her comedy with a knife's edge. As she told a reporter "I've always wanted to be cited for incitement to riot" (Peterson). A subliminal sense of outrage at institutional injustice girds her work, as she prods at patriarchal prejudice in education, religion, politics, and law. An example came at a Clinton concert in Denver in 1995 during the O.J. Simpson trial, when O.J. Simpson was accused of stabbing to death his wife, Nicole Brown, and her friend, Ron Goldman. Of the trial Clinton said, "If Simpson is acquitted, women should riot. And I don't mean politely, I mean overturn and burn cars. Who's thinking of that poor, beaten, dead woman?"

Clinton often jokes about education and about the repressive qualities of Catholicism and fundamentalism. She calls teaching high school "performance art," and teaching English the best preparation for handling drifting audiences. She recalls in her book one day when her students were paying attention to the lawn mower outside and not to her. She left the classroom, hopped on the mower, and waved at her class (81). She says that after being confronted for her innovative lessons by the head of the school board (he accused her of teaching euthanasia in her class on death), she left teaching because of "illness and fatigue. I was sick and tired of it" (82). At the same time in her concerts, she takes time to encourage teachers and to criticize the government for its failure to ultimately support teachers. At the end of her *Read These Lips* concert, she

Feminist Humor and Change 97

asks if there are any teachers in the audience. She directly addresses them as she mocks the false Bush promises for higher teacher pay and lower numbers in each class. She suggests that the promised smaller classes will be good for reading, but it will be "Reading as Fundamentalist."

Kate Clinton enjoys a field day with the political right. She gloats over the fact that Pat Robertson's Christian Coalition lost its tax exempt status, and she suggests that after the killings at Columbine High School the N.R.A. should have been called in to do clean up. At the time of her *Read These Lips* concert, Charleton Heston had just been admitted to the Betty Ford clinic. Clinton gibed: "He's in a new twelve step program—N.R.-A.A." She mocks the intellectual stubbornness of religious literalists when they claim, for example, in the face of incontrovertible scientific evidence, that life began 4,000 years ago. When archeologists unearthed a mastodon 14,000 years old, she says the fundamentalist will say, "That's not a dinosaur. That's a croissant."

Regarding the oppression of the Catholic Church, Clinton is ruthless. In describing "the Polish Pope," she refers to "His Very Narrowness." Because he came to power at the same time as Reagan, she laments: "The Pope and Reagan. Forgive and Forget." In *Read These Lips* she mocks Pope John Paul II for his apologies for past church offenses. When he expressed regret for any role the church *might have had* in the oppression of women, she dismissed it as insincere, offering her own list of offenses for which the Church should apologize, such as bingo and two thousand years of pedophilia. She directs those interested to her new documentary, "Touched by an Archbishop." She also ridicules the Pope for ignoring the institutionalized racism toward the Jews under Pope Pious XII, whom she refers to as "that little shrunken apple head." She describes the Pope as "cloned from a large kielbasa."

As scathing as it is, Clinton's treatment of religion is gentle compared to her treatment of politicians. Commonly in her writing and in her concerts, she lances her victims with caustic taunts: Jesse Helms, "that impotent windsock," Senator Sam Nunn, "Little Miss Fistula," Colin Powell as "The Very Irritable Colin Powell," Michael Dukakis, "Mr. Charisma Bypass," and the "adiposal" Newt Gingrich. Sometimes, as if she can't resist, she reverts to rhyming childhood mockery as in "Norm Norm Big as a Dorm Schwartzkopf."

Calling President George W. Bush our "Commando in Chief" and Secretary of Defense Donald Rumsfeld, "bombilicious Rumsfeld," she "preemptively" formed The Permanent Standing Committee to Impeach Bush, and her concerts and columns often deal with her gripes against the President. One of her biggest issues at the time of the Iraq war was "Patriotic Correctness," in which she felt no one could discuss alternatives to war without being judged as unpatriotic. During the Iraq war she opened a column in *The Advocate* (May 2003) by saying: "I love my country. I hate what's happening. I'm for peace. Since when did saying you're for peace get translated as, 'I think I'll have that darling Saddam over for dinner?'" She called this constant pressure for the patriotic response the "new P.C." After 9/11 she observed that this social pressure to behave politically as expected was like the pressure to stay in the closet, only this time it's a "peace closet."

Her criticism of government crosses the party aisle. She was particularly disappointed that Bill Clinton as President conceded on so many issues, saying "The first strains of 'Inhale to the Chief' had not even died down...[when] he backed up on gays in the military, health care reform, Lani Guinier, welfare reform. Whenever he talked, I swear I could hear that backing-up sound trucks make" (165). Of the election that gave Bill Clinton a second term she said so few people voted, voters were called activists (165). She characterized the discussion on gays in the military as "another circle jerk by the ethically challenged" (126). In 1995 at the end of her ninety-minute performance in her Denver concert, Clinton used hushed tones to address her audience and finished the evening by mocking Bill Clinton's "Don't ask; don't tell" policy regarding gays in the military. She urged her audience, "Ask and tell, NOW MORE THAN EVER!"

As one of the first lesbian comedians and an articulate spokesperson for lesbian issues, Kate Clinton has long held a leadership position in the lesbian community. In 1999, for example, she received the Lifetime Achievement Award from the National Gay and Lesbian Task Force.[4] Because of her sense of history, she articulates many shifts in lesbian comedy through her decades of performance. In an article Clinton wrote for the *Village Voice* in 2002, she suggests that lescoms are allowed to make fun of the patriarchy, and she characterizes their comedy as "bold, bad, and wickedly funny."

Clinton delights that lesbians are attracted to stand-up, not only because it's affordable, but because it celebrates their culture. At the same time she regrets the mainstream's limited tolerance for lesbian humor and notes that many lesbian comedians do not try to be mainstream, but play to an audience primarily made up of lesbian women. "Lesbian humor is uniquely good precisely because it's not in the mainstream. Since it isn't trying to sell anything, it doesn't have to sell out," Clinton asserts in her *Village Voice* article. To a great extent, then, the lescom circuit provides comedians like Clinton with the opportunity to deliver a more open and pungent comedy, because they do not have to negotiate the obstacles and expectations of more conventional mainstream audiences.

In its boldness, brashness, and sexual frankness, a Kate Clinton concert displays impatience if not contempt for middle class feminine values of the accommodating, the polite, and the modest. For example, she ends her *Read These Lips* concert with the quip, "I have Bush fatigue, not the good kind." Her 1995 Denver concert recounted some of the family tensions that her coming out caused: "If you can imagine, my father is 83 and for the first time, this year, he came to my show. He said he was shocked.... He said he has just been having trouble with his heart and I said, 'I think your heart is doing fine if it didn't stop right during the show' " (qtd. in *Out Front* 11).

Feminist Humor and Change 99

As the critic Linda Pershing points out, Clinton also entertains her audiences with bawdy lesbian stories (410). Clinton regaled her Denver audience with the story of how she gained thirty pounds the summer before her senior year in high school, because she fell in love with another waitress at the summer camp where she worked. Since they were both good Catholic girls, they turned their desire for each other toward food, "peach cobbler and chocolate pies, whole chocolate pies" (1995). She told the story with sensory delight: "And we ate Schnecken. Do you know what Schnecken is? I'll tell you. It's this hot, sticky, swirly, caramel, cinnamony bun. Hot...sticky...swirly...cinnamon...BUNS. Do you hear where thirty pounds is happenin'?"

Throughout a Clinton concert there is a sense of frankness about lesbian sexuality, not for its shock value, but as an honest presentation of a joyful part of lesbian life. Her sexual jokes convey not only a sense of daring, but also a sense of fun. While asking in *Read These Lips* whether Ellen DeGeneres' former girlfriend, Anne Heche, was ever really gay, Clinton suggests that since the lesbian community is so small, they would have known if Anne Heche had dated a woman. "If you laid all the lesbians end to end—what a weekend!"

CLINTON'S TECHNIQUE

Clinton achieves her artistic success in a tightly structured format—little is random, little ad-libbed. She claims she over prepares, a habit developed writing lesson plans as a teacher. The concerts are ninety minutes long, longer than most stand-up concerts, and they have a definite beginning and end. Clinton begins her concerts with, "Thanks for coming out!" Clinton relates that her first manager was a former music manager who suggested to Clinton the standard music practice was a forty-five minute set, followed by another forty-five minute set. Clinton adopted that practice, even though it has proved rigorous. As much a writer as a comedian, Clinton writes her own material and hones it as she travels to various cities six months out of every year. Her concerts presume a certain level of awareness on the part of her audience as she refers to current political figures, social patterns, and even American history. She disdains dumbing down in comedy and feels that her audience wants to be challenged mentally. "One of the most sexy parts of the body is the brain," Clinton remarked in an interview with *Womankind*. Her audience is loyal and will brave many obstacles to see her concerts. For example, the night of the January 1995 concert in Denver was harsh and stormy and the organizers didn't know whether to hold the concert or not. Clinton told them: "Don't worry; my audience will be here; they drive four wheelers." The audience was full, even though many other events had been cancelled, and she laughed with her audience in celebration of tenacity.

From the beginning of her career, Clinton has respected the power of laughter. "I think humor is very dangerous," she told *Womankind*. Rather than seeing humor as diversionary, Clinton believes that humor helps lighten heavy issues so people can move through them. "There is like a window of vulnerability. They [the audience] laugh about things they maybe never would, and in that laughing the things come into them and they think," she told the *Womankind* reporter. As a feminist who is working for revolutionary change in the political and social system, Clinton thinks humor can bear the load, by reversing its weight. She is committed for many more years to using her well honed skills as a performer and writer to make people laugh and think.

PAULA POUNDSTONE: DOMESTIC COMEDY SERVED UP BY A POLITICAL WIT

Of her own career track Paula Poundstone has said, "I'm just amazed that what I got thrown out of class for, I now get paid to do."[5] Poundstone, whose appeal is more mainstream than that of Kate Clinton, mixes a brand of devilish domestic humor with a political and social critique. That she is unique among comedians was emphasized by Billy Crystal when he introduced her in the first *Comic Relief* (1986): "She's a fantastic comedian. She's very innovative; she's very eccentric, off beat, she's bizarre, and she's one of the best comedians out there today." That characterization may have been sparked by Poundstone's strikingly casual onstage manner. In contrast to many other comedians, she bonds with the audience by engaging them occasionally in conversation. Despite the apparent randomness of her comic routine, her concerts leave a sense of gentle provocation. From her unusual blend of the domestic and political she sparks thought as well as laughter.

Born in 1959 in Massachusetts, Poundstone is one of the many comedians who came up in the '80s. She has spent most of her career touring to comedy clubs, colleges, and special groups across the country, but she has also been a committed performer on comedy shows dedicated to social causes, such as *Comic Relief*. A frequent guest on television's *The Tonight Show* and *The Rosie O'Donell Show*, she briefly hosted her own television show and has been a regular panelist on the syndicated quiz show *To Tell the Truth*.[6] Her 1992 HBO Special, "Cats, Cops, and Stuff," won a Cable Ace Award, and she has also won an American Comedy Award as "Best Female Stand-up" as well as a local Emmy.

Her comedy has been sought for national events, including backstage commentary on the '93 Emmys and commentary on the '94 Oscars. Poundstone has also been recognized for her humor writing. From 1993–1998 she wrote "The Poundstone Report" for *Mother Jones* magazine, where she mixed her gentle observational humor with searing political wit. She has also written for *The Los Angeles Times, Sunday Calendar, Entertainment Weekly*, and *Buzz Magazine*.

POUNDSTONE'S PERFORMANCE

To the *Las Vegas Sun*, Poundstone described her work: "My act is largely biographical, what I'm thinking, what I'm doing. I have never kept a secret before in my life." At one point in her routine she jokes about achieving her dream of working at the International House of Pancakes: "When people would be rude to me, I would touch their eggs." (qtd. in *Wisecracks*). In a Denver show, she joked about the trouble indifference toward sex has caused her. When she says, "I don't like sex," a common response is, "Well, you will with me" (1996). As a single mother, Poundstone finds humor in her domestic life, which focuses on raising children and pets. Her stories will often drift into very ordinary discussions of daily household decisions, as when she discussed whether or not to buy her toddler a kitten, "The thing is, I already have six cats and two bunnies, but the cats are mine, and the bunnies used to be cute but now they're huge and ugly and frumpy, and I don't trust them" ("Paula Poundstone" 1996). She puts on one of her extremely varied facial expressions to punctuate her remark.

Like Phyllis Diller and Roseanne, this major comedian focuses on domestic life, but rather than deliver a series of prepared jokes as Diller did, Poundstone weaves in and out of domestic subjects as she weaves across the stage, telling stories and illuminating ironies. While Diller made fun of herself for being unable to meet the expectations for the conventional wife and mother, Poundstone makes fun of herself for being unable to meet the expectations for an unconventional mother. She was a foster mother from 1993–2001, mostly of newborns, and has been an advocate for foster children, encouraging more people to adopt. Poundstone has three adopted children.

Poundstone's domestic life was the object of media attention when in June of 2001 she was arrested by the Santa Monica police and pleaded guilty to charges of felony child endangerment and misdemeanor child injury. Her foster children were removed, and she was sentenced to 180 days in alcohol rehabilitation and five years probation. Her adopted children were forbidden to sleep at the house for a time. Poundstone and her attorney say that the charge stems from her taking a trip with the children to the ice cream parlor when she was drunk, which she told a *San Francisco Chronicle* reporter was "colossally stupid."

Committed to honesty, Poundstone did not try to hide these events, but referred to them in her act as she bridged from her troubled personal life back into her performance career. In a Santa Cruz performance, she addressed the audience about her rehab: "It's kind of strange to see this many seats not in a circle" (Sullivan). After cautiously reentering stand-up in California venues, Poundstone has gradually continued her nationwide stand-up tours. To a Washington, D.C. audience, she referred to her excessive drinking problem. She said she should have known she had a problem when she added a new puppy to her entourage of nine cats. "Believe me, the cats were hiding the liquor after that" (Toto). Humor and heartbreak come together in this joke to an interviewer about the terms of her sentence, forbidding her from ever adopting again: "So every time I drive past one of the Adopt-A-Highway signs, I say, 'No not me. That's for others'" (Lipton).

In her efforts to reclaim her comedy career, Poundstone brings strong factors to work in her favor: rapport with her audience and political wit. Of her 2002 stand-up act in Washington, D.C. a skeptical reviewer, unimpressed with both her domestic material and her frankness about her court trouble, begrudgingly concluded: "The Warner Theatre crowd instantly forgave her, chortling through the rambling set" (Toto). It is not surprising that Poundstone reliably formed a relationship with the crowd. "My shows have a feeling of being in the living room with a bunch of friends," she says of her own work.[7]

POUNDSTONE'S TECHNIQUE

Several strategies make her audience rapport possible: quickness, casualness, and interaction. In a live performance she will address the audience directly in questions and respond to anyone who answers her. If someone heckles, she is more likely to joke with the lone voice than she is to scold. From these audience interchanges she makes spontaneous jokes, rare among comedians. She told a reporter for *Time* that up to thirty percent of her act is ad lib (Kanfer).

Poundstone uses the stand-up's conventional stool for more than a water holder. She wraps herself around it, crawls over it, and even lies down with her back on the floor. Sometimes she drips her whole body over the stage as she speaks. Despite the unconventionality of this, her personal manner is completely non-threatening, even self-deprecating. In an article for *Mother Jones*, titled "Keeping My Mouth Shut," she discusses the difficulty she has always had with asserting herself. When she was thirteen at the doctor's office, for example, her mother had to keep the nurse from locking up the office, because Poundstone was still in the examining room inside. She paints a poignant picture of a shy teenager alone in the examination room, unable to ask to see the doctor. In another article for *Mother Jones*, "Be Like Gandhi," she tells how she values small daily kindnesses, like letting people into traffic, even though these values are neither rewarded nor emulated.

By contrast to her gentle manner, her political humor is piercing. When she was a correspondent for the Republican Convention in 1996, a reporter asked her what she would wear. She said she would have to have her hair lifted to fit in. In her *Mother Jones* column she made a detailed comparison of the Republican Arianna Huffington to a guinea pig. In the article "Field Guide to Republicans," she repeatedly quoted the guinea pig section in order to fathom Huffington's self-important behavior: "The lead female strives for rank among her contemporaries."

Feminist Humor and Change 103

Poundstone has been a political activist who, after Colorado passed Amendment 2, the anti-gay legislation, considered boycotting the state, as so many other stars were doing. Rather than cancel, she added jokes about the intolerance of the religious right. Still concerned in a Denver performance in 1995 with the religious right's dominance in Colorado Springs, she told a story to a Denver audience about interviewing Will Perkins, the leader of the group, "Colorado for Family Values,"

> He said he knows all about discrimination because he's a car salesman and people make fun of his plaid pants and white shoes. He was absolutely serious. Maybe I'm naive, but I don't think he knows he's mean. He thinks he's a perfectly nice guy.

Still referring to Colorado Springs as its own right-wing entity, in her 1996 Denver show, she said of Colorado, "You have three cities, Denver, Boulder, and Aspen. And then there's Colorado Springs." To get away with these gibes, Poundstone typically places her domestic material before her political material, presumably to cushion the strong viewpoint of her political material, which makes no attempt to accommodate conservative listeners. For example, in an interview for the film about female stand-ups, *Wisecracks*, Poundstone says of Republicans: "I'll never make enough money to be that big an asshole."

Paula Poundstone stands out as a contemporary comedian who rarely talks about sex or calls any attention to her own body. The family of her comedy is nothing like the fictional family of Diller's creation, in that Poundstone talks about her real children and pets. By contrast, her political material ridicules incompetence, stupidity, and intolerance. She particularly challenges her audience to rethink growing acceptance of political and social intolerance. Her potion stings, but Paula Poundstone provides the laughter to drink it down.

WHOOPI GOLDBERG: A COMEDY WITH SOCIAL JUSTICE

Few comedians can match the cultural impact of Whoopi Goldberg. The range and depth of her successes, along with her high visibility, work in multiple genres, and outspokenness on social justice, have changed the landscape for women and comedy in significant ways. She has been a stand-up, an award-winning performer in one-woman shows on Broadway and in television, a writer and producer, and has been a frequent host of many entertainment shows, including *Comic Relief* and The Academy Awards. A testimony to her popularity was her selection to host the 2002 Academy Awards. With the wounds of the nation still raw after 9/11, Whoopi Goldberg was called upon to extend her trademark combination of fun and fire, warmth and truth to lighten the nation's grief.

Despite her accomplishments, she firmly rejects labels, particularly those of "female comedian" and "African-American." As she told an interviewer, "There's no way to pigeonhole me because my interests are too widespread, and I don't live under any mental restrictions."[8] Consistent in her work, however, is her commitment to causes of feminism, poverty, and race. Though sometimes criticized as too outspoken, she sustains popular support through her unique personal magnetism, her willingness to laugh at herself, and her insightful honesty.

Born in 1955, Goldberg grew up in a housing project in Chelsea district of New York City. She and her brother were raised by a single mom, who worked as a nurse. Educated by nuns in elementary school, Goldberg later rejected the angry God she encountered there, choosing instead to believe in a God of kindness (Bonavoglia 115). From ages eight to ten she acted in plays at the Hudson's Guild Children's Theatre, but she was always attracted to character actors in television movies and was particularly fond of horror tales. When she was thirteen she dropped out of school and struggled with drug addiction as a young teen.

Growing up in the '60s, she participated in street protests against the Viet Nam war and she protested at Columbia University. As a teenager she appeared on Broadway in the choruses of *Hair*, *Jesus Christ Superstar*, and *Pippin*, before moving to California at nineteen with her baby daughter. In San Diego she helped found the San Diego Repertory Theatre and joined the improvisational group, "Spontaneous Combustion." Though named Caryn Johnson at birth, she invented her stage name, "Whoopi," as a joke about her flatulence. To stabilize the name, she added the last name "Goldberg," a tribute to her mixed ethnic heritage. Throughout these early years, she supported herself and her infant daughter by working in the theatre, as a bricklayer, and as a hairdresser for a mortician. To make ends meet she was also on welfare. In her book she discusses her lack of shame for having to get aid from the government (130–2).

Her solo performance career began one night when her stand-up partner was unable to perform. Though she went on stage alone and reluctantly, she realized for the first time that she could successfully entertain a San Francisco audience for an hour. Goldberg moved then from Southern California to Berkeley and began developing one-woman shows, creating a monologue show with four characters, *The Spook Show*. In 1984, Goldberg accepted an invitation to do the show as part of a workshop at the Dance Theatre Workshop in Manhattan. When Mike Nichols, the esteemed actor and producer, saw the show, he asked to produce it on Broadway. Before Goldberg accepted the offer, she returned to California to perform in *Moms*, a one-woman show that she had written with Ellen Sebastian, about the black comedian Moms Mabley. Goldberg then returned to New York to open her Broadway show, now entitled, *Whoopi Goldberg*, to which she had added two characters. The show was

Feminist Humor and Change 105

taped before it closed on Broadway, and the film version became a 1985 television special, *Whoopi Goldberg: Direct from Broadway*, which was awarded a Grammy.[9]

GOLDBERG: FILM AND TELEVISION

Goldberg's wide-ranging film career was launched in the mid-'80s when Mike Nichols insisted that Stephen Spielberg consider Whoopi Goldberg for a role in his upcoming film, *The Color Purple*. Based on Alice Walker's novel, the film unfolds the story of a poor black girl in the South who breaks away from her abusive older husband and grows into a confident woman through the mentoring and love of another woman. Goldberg had already written to Alice Walker asking for a role, saying she would take any part, because she so admired the novel. Goldberg auditioned for Spielberg and several others in his living room, where she performed for him her Broadway show. Clearly impressed, Spielberg cast Goldberg as Celie, the lead, and in 1986 Goldberg received an Oscar nomination for Best Actress in a Leading Role and a Golden Globe Award. The production of the film stirred controversy in the black community, however. Critics objected that the producers were not also black. Goldberg nonetheless continued to significantly increase her visibility. In 1986, Goldberg co-hosted the television special *Comic Relief* with Robin Williams and Billy Crystal.

Goldberg's film career was cemented when she won the 1991 Oscar for Best Actress in a Supporting Role for her work as the smart talking medium in the film *Ghost*. This was followed by many other box office hits including *Sister Act* (1992) and *Sister Act 2* (1993). She has also appeared in serious films, such as *Sarafina!* (1992), *How Stella Got Her Groove Back* (1998), and *Girl Interrupted* (1999). Her distinctive voice has been heard in many movies as well, including the notable 1994 film *The Lion King*, in which she played a hyena. This extensive film career resulted in her being the highest-paid actress in Hollywood during the early '90s.[10]

Goldberg has kept an equally high profile on television as a comedian and actress. Beginning in 1987 she starred in many episodes of *Star Trek: The Next Generation*. She was nominated by the American Comedy Awards as the Funniest Female Performer in a TV Special for *Comic Relief VIII* (1998) and *The 71st Annual Academy Awards* (1999). *Hollywood Squares*, a show she produced and in which she starred for four seasons, was nominated for a Daytime Emmy each year from 1999–2002. In 2002 she received the American Film Institute's Star Award, which recognizes individuals for excellence in film and television. Previous winners include Robin Williams and Billy Crystal.[11] Her myriad television and film commitments did not keep her from returning to Broadway, however. In 2003 she produced and starred in *Ma Rainey's Black Bottom*, August Wilson's play about the famous blues singer Ma Rainey, and in

1997 she replaced Nathan Lane on Broadway in *A Funny Thing Happened on the Way to the Forum*.[12] Of her multi-dimensional career Goldberg told a reporter for *Daily Variety*, "Looking back, I had a lot more gumption than I thought. But I don't know where it comes from. I'd bottle it if I did" (Maynard).

GOLDBERG'S SOCIAL VIEWS: FEMINISM, POVERTY, AND RACISM

Goldberg on Feminism

Goldberg has used her prominence to highlight many social issues including women's rights. In the spring of 2003 she appeared on the cover of *Ms.* magazine in a tee shirt that read, "This Is What Feminism Looks Like." Her feminist views, though consistent, have always been singular. In 1986, when interviewed on *The Today Show*, she said that the reason she insists upon being called an "actor" and not an "actress" is that "An actress can only play a woman. I'm an actor. I can play anything" (qtd. in *Ms*. 59). She was vindicated when she stepped into Nathan Lane's role in *Forum* and was credited with being the first actress to take a male actor's role on Broadway.[13] In her 1984 Broadway show, she played four women and two men with equal ease. She has also been an outspoken advocate for reproductive choice in abortion and, with her characteristic honesty, has discussed her own abortion as a fourteen-year-old in the book *The Choices We Made: 25 Women and Men Speak Out About Abortion*. She says that she created the character of the fourteen-year-old valley girl to underscore how desperately young pregnant girls need help. In the girl, who inflicts a damaging abortion on herself with a coat hanger, Goldberg hoped that parents might see their own children, and be more apt to listen (Bonavoglia 117). Goldberg added, "I made the character white, because nobody would have given a fuck about a poor woman of color—that's the bottom line" (118).

Goldberg on Poverty and Homelessness

Goldberg has also used her celebrity status to draw attention to issues of poverty and homelessness. In her book, *Book*, she states her views on the discrepancy between the rich and the poor: "I want to see the space between rich and poor narrowed in my time on this planet" (136). When she joined Billy Crystal and Robin Williams in 1986 to host the first *Comic Relief*, they earned $2.5 million in pledges for homeless projects throughout America. The 1986 *Comic Relief* curtain opens on the cardboard shelters of many homeless. Robin Williams crawls out of one box and introduces himself to Whoopi's character as a farmer who has lost his holdings. Whoopi's homeless character complains of her mistreatment at the Welfare Office where an officer had called all homeless "bums and winos." Whoopi replies: "I ain't no bum, I'm on hard times." In her book, Goldberg shows sustained compassion for those on welfare and the poor: "Here's what I know: folks at the bottom rungs are having a rough time pulling themselves up to a better place, and folks up top aren't always reaching down to lend a helping hand" (127). She has repeatedly demonstrated her commitment to homeless issues by hosting *Comic Relief* in 1989, 1991, 1992, 1994, 1995, and 1998.

The biting political satire of *Comic Relief* reflects Goldberg's views on poverty and government. In the 1986 show, Robin Williams portrays Ronald Reagan watching Nancy put on a designer dress. He quips, "Mother, you can either wear that or feed Cleveland." Later, Billy Crystal interviews Robin Williams as William F. Buckley and asks him to analyze the Reagan administration. Referring to Reagan's "trickle down" theory of economics, Williams says, "The poor are really being pissed on."

Comic Relief III takes this view even further. It opens with a gala musical number in which Goldberg, Williams, and Crystal, dressed in tuxedoes, dance and sing "Over Here," a parody of the patriotic World War I song, "Over There." One of the lines states: "Don't buy a brand new fax, don't pay your income tax, send it over here." Robin Williams asks the audience to join them in the singing by following the bouncing head of Vice President Dan Quayle. Quayle's smiling head then bounces over the lyrics flashed on the screen. At the end of the show a huge billboard descends with Uncle Sam in his traditional garb saying, "I Want You... To Give." By 1996, the Comic Relief organization advertised that it had sent pledges to twenty-five homeless projects in twenty-three cities.

Goldberg on Race

Goldberg's views on race are equally intense, but just as she resists being called a "woman comedian," she expresses fierce resistance to being called African-American. "Call me an asshole, call me a blowhard, but don't call me an African American. Please" (Goldberg 105). She clarifies this stance in *Book*, stating that racial labeling separates people and that we should get beyond skin color. "When you tell the story of this country, I'm part of the fabric. Black people, stop trying to identify elsewhere" (113).

Goldberg has been a leading actor to bring focus to black history. She narrated the HBO documentary *Unchained Memories* (2003), which profiles slave narratives. Her Broadway work on Ma Rainey highlights the life of a singularly talented blues singer who fought against racial and economic prejudice. Goldberg narrated the television show *Beyond Tara*, which showcased the work of black actress Hattie McDaniel, who won an Academy Award for her role as the maid in the film *Gone With the Wind*. Goldberg was herself the first black woman since Hattie McDaniel to win an Academy Award. Goldberg somewhat reluctantly played a maid in the film *The Long Walk Home*, which tells the behind the scenes story of the Montgomery bus boycott. However, after talking to black women who had struggled though those hard times as best they could, she related better to the maid role, understanding that it was not demeaning, but a means of survival.[14]

On the issue of racial injustice, Goldberg's stand-up has been searing and political. An example was her 1991 HBO Special, *Chez Whoopi*, which deals with L.A.'s disruption by riots, Darryl Gates as former Police Chief, and Clarence Thomas as a nominee for the Supreme Court. In her stand-up, she affirms African-American culture, ridicules racism in the dominant white society, and exhorts her audience toward political action and hope in a future of change. Goldberg's idiom and her attitude of defiance toward the racism of the white culture imbue her stand-up with some of the qualities intrinsic to ethnic humor (Dresner 183). Goldberg set up this special in an African-American neighborhood in South Central Los Angeles, the Crenshaw neighborhood, and the audience was predominantly black. Throughout the special, she used this setting to celebrate difference and to encourage black pride:

> We decided we wanted to do our HBO show in the neighborhood. It was really interesting when I told HBO where I wanted to do the show. Caucasian folks get very nervous when there's a bunch of us congregated. Well, here we are down in the Crenshaw. We look very good! (*Chez Whoopi*).

Goldberg underlined black solidarity by ridiculing situations where blacks are expected to live with a double standard of justice. In the following narrative, she celebrates the dismissal of former L.A. Police Chief Darryl Gates, who had been publicly accused of racism: "But now that Darryl Gates is gone, I feel a lot better on the street.... People been saying this shit for two years [that Gates was racist], they should have read the Goldberg report. Cause it's one page: FUCK HIM!"

A subtext of the evening was L.A. police brutality, some of which had been caught on videotape and used as evidence against Gates. Despite the tragedy attendant on the violence, there was a sense of vindication among black people that Goldberg celebrated:

> Sony is really thrilled about all of this that's come down. Because now brothers are going out and buying cameras and saying to cops, "Yeah, mother fuckers, come on. Yeah, I'm shooting your ass now. Hit him!" Beta cam, beta cam, never leave home without it (*Chez Whoopi*).

As the evening went on, Goldberg expressed her political views more strongly by ridiculing the system of Supreme Court appointments and nominee Clarence Thomas:

> The Supreme Court's kinda scary. They're tryin' to be real slick, tryin' to bring a brother in. Right! This mother fucker shows up wearin' a hood. He doesn't believe in Equal Opportunity. How does he think he got where he was?" (*Chez Whoopi*).

At this point, Goldberg urges specific political action against Thomas to keep him out of the Supreme Court:

> "I'm sayin', "No!" I'm . . . sendin' telegrams. You send telegrams: 'No! Not this one.' I don't care if he's black.' That doesn't mean shit. Do not let this mother fucker in the Supreme Court or we all goin' home" (*Chez Whoopi*).

Despite the painful accounting of what she perceived as growing racism in the country and in the world ("It's open season on black folks around the world"), Goldberg asserted the importance of each individual and the importance of taking a political stand: "But I'm keepin' the faith. I'm keepin' hope. I think it's gonna get better. Because I think it's important for us to say, 'Yeah, yeah for us!' Not just black people, but as people, 'cause we livin' in weird times, strange times. We're not gonna let that [growth of racism] happen. I'm not gonna let that happen." There was a sense that she was on a mission against despair and against further embattlement between the races. While frankly acknowledging the daily injuries of racism, Goldberg built the show to a joyful climax, calling upon neighborhood and racial pride. She ended the show urging communication between adults and young people. Black teenagers flooded the stage as she said, "It's important to remember that the future is in the young people of the country. . . . If we can continue to encourage them, you never know where they're gonna show up." She then introduces the teenagers as the "Crenshaw High School Choir" and asks the audience to view them as an example of what America can be and why it's important to keep a dialogue open with youth. The show ends when the chorus sings, "America, the Beautiful."

In the hands of almost any other comedian, this ending of the show would have been trite, but from Whoopi Goldberg who understands the destructive power of systemic racism, it was a very hopeful gesture. Goldberg's bolstering of black pride has much in common with comedian Kate Clinton's celebration of identity for her lesbian constituency. A significant difference is Goldberg's star status, which assures her a national audience for her views. Goldberg demonstrates a unique use of women's comedy as secular revival, where the comedian witnesses with her audience painful cultural truths, uses humor to offset the ironies and injustices of racism, but chooses, nonetheless, to underline positive community values and leave her audience with a spirit of hope for future possibility.

Goldberg's Technique

How does Whoopi Goldberg so convincingly take on so many characters in so many genres? Few actors have moved so seamlessly from the stand-up stage to Broadway to film to television, and back to Broadway. Goldberg first manifested her virtuosity in her one-woman show, *Whoopi Goldberg*. In that show, consisting of monologues with six characters, she demonstrated a method of creating characters effortlessly, as if her body were their bodies. Witnesses to the live performance called it "magical," "eerie," and "the gift of tongues." (qtd. in *Current Biography*). Her method echoes Lily Tomlin's "comedic possession," and has the same shamanistic form with the parallel purpose of both delighting an audience and broadening its experience to include characters normally dismissed. In an interview with Harry Haun for show's *Playbill*, Goldberg said, "… I see myself as a medium, something from which these people spring" (146). She says that she did not write down the lines for the characters, but that she kept them living in her head—something she considered the job of the actor. Although this interview took place in the mid-'80s, Goldberg was still using this technique through the late '90s, because her intuitive method gave her trouble as she tried to write her book, *Book* (1997). "Most people put pen to paper, but I've never been that kind of writer. I have to work my shit out on my feet, and then, after I've done it, I can finally set it down. But that's not how you write a book" (Goldberg 236). For the stage, her method of bringing characters to life in her head endows them with a depth and humanity.

In her one-woman show *Whoopi Goldberg*, each of the six characters comes alive in spirit and resonates as a living person. This is achieved not only through her expert acting skills and precise accents, but through her compassion for the distinct spirit by which each character achieves his/her humanity. This visceral knowledge of their humanity allows Goldberg to travel as if by magic from young to old, black to white, and male to female in the show. The characters are bound together, not by race or gender, but by the vulnerability of human beings as they try to negotiate the tough obstacles of life. When Goldberg transforms into a developmentally disabled young woman, she presents a character with human needs and a disdain for pity. The thirteen-year-old white girl who gives herself an abortion with a coat hanger is much worse off than the little black girl who wishes she had blond hair. The Jamaican woman character, who lives in as the cook, cleaning woman, and occasional lover of an old rich white man, has a firmer grasp on reality than does Fontaine, her streetwise junkie with a Ph.D. Even Fontaine manages to invite the audience into the complexities of his life. Goldberg's insight into the inner life of the character frees them from stereotype and extends the audience's experience into lives usually unseen.

Goldberg's virtuosity combines a unique set of acting skills with a personal belief in the possibilities of human beings. Before her stardom, she

Feminist Humor and Change 111

expressed this belief to a Broadway audience when she spoke with them after a performance of *Whoopi Goldberg*, a conversation recorded in the video of the show. She encouraged her audience to dream, because she said it's possible to achieve dreams. Who in Chelsea, she asked, would have believed that "little Whoop" would make it to Broadway? Her confidence and sense of fun in whatever work she undertakes allow her to project a powerful magnetism that fills her work with spirit. Testimony to this is her plethora of awards, including the People's Choice Award for Favorite Comedy Motion Picture Actress in 1993, 1994, and 1995.[15] When Mike Nichols, who can be credited with discovering Goldberg, was interviewed by Harry Haun for *Playbill* he said, "Her compassion and her humanity are enormously moving and quite startling in someone that funny" (qtd. in *Current Biography*). Outstanding talent, optimism, the strength of her character work, and a belief in the possibility of a just world combine to make Whoopi Goldberg's work uniquely powerful among women in comedy.

Kate Clinton, Paula Poundstone, and Whoopi Goldberg show the power of comedy by using their talent, wit, and experience to shed light on some of the most troubling social and political issues of the nation. Though sometimes controversial, they have not backed down and diluted their views. Their acts all show agreement with Kate Clinton when she said to a reporter for *Capital Xtra!*, "I think it's important to create a show where people feel comfortable and uncomfortable." These women do not hesitate to give a little jolt with their laughter. Following in the feminist tradition, Margaret Cho creates a comedy calling for more tolerance for gays, people of color, and standards of female beauty. Her blasts of comedy contrast with the more mainstream comedy of Ellen Generes, whose gentle observational humor highlights life's ironies.

Chapter Seven

Margaret Cho and Ellen DeGeneres

Directions for Women in Stand-Up

AS THE ARC OF WOMEN IN COMEDY EXTENDS ACROSS THE CENTURY, certain developments are notable. The foundation of the arc is strong, thanks to the pioneering work of comedians like Phyllis Diller, Lily Tomlin, and Roseanne. Other women will add to the sweep of this arc, each with her distinctive voice. Many will continue the tradition of women as satirists; others will steer a gentler path. As two of the most prominent comedians of the late twentieth and early twenty-first centuries, Margaret Cho and Ellen DeGeneres each define different directions for women's stand-up. Their career paths, however, are remarkably similar and reflect those of stand-ups, like Jerry Seinfeld, who have reached celebrity status. Both came up through comedy clubs, gained national recognition for excellence in their stand-up acts, and then were asked to join the increasing number of comedians who have starred in television sitcoms.[1] Both had their shows cancelled to great personal disappointment. Cho's show, *All American Girl* (1994), played for one season; DeGeneres' show, *Ellen* (1993–1997), was cancelled after five years amidst a media frenzy when both she and her television character came out as gay. Both women have been in several films and both have written books. Cho's book, *I'm the One That I Want,* grew out of her successful concert by the same name and chronicles the devastating personal effects of the cancellation of her television show. *My Point...And I Do Have One*, DeGeneres' book, relates her observations of daily life.

Both women continue to write and to perform in national comedy tours, which then are typically produced in film and DVD. Two of Cho's shows, *I'm the One That I Want* (2000) and *Notorious C.H.O.* (2002) were self-produced and distributed; *Notorious C.H.O.* was also distributed as an independent film. DeGeneres has had a history of producing HBO comedy specials, and she has been the executive producer on her last two concerts, which became HBO specials: *The Beginning* (2000) and *Here and Now* (2003).

Despite their similar career trajectories, each woman has a unique and contrasting approach to her material and, as a consequence, attracts a different audience. Following in the tradition of the feminist comedians, Cho rages against the inequities of the dominant culture, particularly in the ways it seeks to devalue gays, people of color, and women. Her sexually frank material carries a shock value, a la Richard Pryor. For example, she opens her *Notorious C.H.O.* concert by suggesting that she's done her part for New York after 9/11 by visiting Ground Zero and giving blow jobs to rescue workers. Though her bawdy comedy lacks mainstream appeal, it attracts a large audience of gays, Asian-Americans, women, and the young and hip.

By contrast, Ellen DeGeneres presents herself as an apolitical comedian whose audience is middle-class American and whose comedy is basic and clean. In a 2002 interview with Terry Gross for *Fresh Air*, DeGeneres said, "I'm not a political person, I'm not an activist and I kind of got sucked into that role just . . . by being honest about my sexuality." However, this statement shows a change from her position during the period from 1997–2000 when DeGeneres was an activist for gay rights, coming out in 1997 on the cover of *Time*, and receiving an award in 2000 from Amnesty International for her "personal commitment to help others secure equal, fair, and humane treatment around the world."[2] The award notes her high profile participation in the memorial to honor the memory of Matthew Shepherd, who had been brutally murdered in Wyoming for being gay. Her concert *The Beginning* (2000) also manifests a shift to an edgier comedy. In this concert DeGeneres somewhat modifies her girl-next-door image and replaces it with a persona who is clearly vulnerable, a person disappointed at the homophobic treatment she received after coming out. A portion of this concert confronts gay issues. Her 2003 concert, *Here and Now*, reclaims her position as a proponent of clean, issue-free comedy, by emphasizing everyday subjects and observational humor, thus targeting a broad middle-class audience. Even though DeGeneres has decided to be open about her sexuality, she has never been a frankly sexual comedian and, especially in contrast to Cho, appears increasingly desirous of maintaining a clear boundary between her personal life and her comedy.

MARGARET CHO

Born in San Francisco in 1968, Cho went to first and second grades on Haight Street, among, as she describes in her book, hippies, ex-druggies, drag queens, and Chinese people (Cho 8). In high school her best friends were two drag queens, and she still calls herself a "fag-hag," one who prefers the company of gay men. After dropping out of high school, Cho worked at her parents' bookstore by day and at San Francisco comedy clubs by night (71). In 1991 she moved to L.A. to hone her comedy and commit to stand-up. From 1991 to 1994, Cho traveled throughout California and the country doing her comedy act, soon becoming the most booked act in the college circuit and winning the 1994 American Comedy Award for Female Comedian. Recognition led to television appearances on television shows for Jerry Seinfeld, Arsenio Hall, and a spot on Bob Hope's prime time special (Kelly 115).

In 1994 Cho starred in *All American Girl*, ABC's experimental sitcom featuring the first Asian-American family on television. Deemed "too ethnic" by some network managers and "not authentic" by some in the Asian-American community, the show was cancelled after one season. In her autobiography, Cho describes the attendant chaos, confusion, and media controversy (130).

In keeping with her ideal of making the personal public, Cho has created intriguing comedy from the disaster of her show's cancellation. Immense talent, good writing, vulnerability, and a commanding approach to sensitive cultural issues have made her concerts enormous successes. Her off-Broadway show, *I'm the One That I Want*, was named as one of the "Great performances of the Year," by *Entertainment Weekly* and won the *New York Magazine* "Performance of the Year" award (Kelly 116).

As a comedian committed to cultural change, Cho can be brutally honest. In her book *I'm the One That I Want*, she asserts that she can never get too personal. "We all have ...horrible things that have happened to us that shouldn't have, and when we cover them up and try to pretend that everything is okay, then our stories are forgotten, and our truths become lies" (166). To a great degree her comedy turns on shock at her openness and her brash manner. After referring to her period in the film *Notorious C.H.O.*, she does an imitation of a man having his period, frenzied by his ravenous appetite and wild emotional swings. He is particularly inconvenienced that Super Bowl Sunday occurs on day two, his heavy flow day.

Cho often confesses something private or vulnerable about herself and uses that to introduce an observation and make a point. Her concert *I'm the One That I Want* details her rampage into self-destruction after the cancellation of her sitcom. Her high degree of honesty lends credibility to her attacks on the television producers for their insensitivity to race and for their crushing adherence to a stereotyped standard of female beauty. Her concert describes how a trainer worked her out four hours a day, six days a week. "I lost weight through dieting, through exercise, but mostly through fear. My kidneys collapsed."

Like Roseanne, Cho is a warrior for her point of view and her voice. When Cho's television character, also a stand-up, was criticized for making fun of her Korean family in her act, ABC pulled back the family criticism. Cho had always made gentle fun of her mother's Korean accent and some of her protective attitudes, and without this dimension Cho felt the episodes became diluted. Quentin Tarantino, whom she was dating at the time, urged her to fight back: "They took away your voice! Don't let them do that! You fucking live to publicly embarrass your family!!!" (qtd. in Cho 131). Cho's live concerts also address the issue of finding one's voice and using it not only to benefit oneself but also to redress some of the power imbalances in the world. Cho's stand-up demonstrates a firm commitment to use her comic voice to claim a place for those marginalized by the culture. On the subject of injustice towards gays, race, and women her comedy is as angry as it is funny.

CHO ON GAYS

Cho devotes a considerable portion of each concert to the exploration and celebration of gay culture. She interacts directly with the gays in the audience, and she tries to include them in all her subjects. "I love the word faggot, because it describes my kind of guy. I am a fag-hag. ...We went to the prom with you" (*I'm the One That I Want*, DVD). When she switches to topics of straight sex, she tells the gays in the audience that she'll get back to them. While these routines exude a great sense of playfulness, she also uses them to shed light on the patriarchy. She notes the terrible looking men in heterosexual porn and wonders aloud if the creators of straight porn are deliberately choosing ugly men, so that straight men viewers can avoid having "a homo moment." She claims that if she were not able to talk to gay men, she wouldn't talk to any men, because she's scared of heterosexual men. She frankly admires the playfulness of gay sexuality and enjoys the outrageousness of the culture. Prior to her *Notorious* concert, filmed at Carnegie Hall, Cho admitted that she loved the idea of bringing into the revered establishment a "queer, tattooed, hipster" audience instead of its usual highbrow music lovers.

CHO ON RACE

A Korean-American, Cho uses her unique position as stand-up to turn the issue of race for both comedy and comment. When asked by the *Houston Chronicle* how much of her audience is Asian, she estimated thirty percent (McDaniel). When asked by the same reporter if she aspired to change the general public's perspective of Asian people, Cho answered, "I would like to. Or add to whatever the social and cultural makeup of an Asian woman is."

In *I'm the One That I Want*, Cho tells of driving through Tennessee when she was on the road in her early days: "You don't want to drive through Tennessee when you look like this. I got to know the Ku Klux Klan way too well. I don't mean to judge them, but they're assholes." Cho also makes fun of the "Asian expert" who was hired to help her become more Asian for her television show. "Margaret, use chop sticks. When you are done, put them in your hair." Cho recalls how early in her career, she was rejected by one agent who told her that Asians could not succeed in the entertainment industry. She adds that later, when her show was cancelled, one of her managers said, "The Asian thing puts people off." Cho's response: "What is 'the Asian Thing'? Some gimmick that I pull out of my ass every couple of years to jazz up my career?" (Cho 203). In *Notorious C.H.O.* she jokes about the effects on a rising star of never having seen Asian people on TV. "I would dream: Maybe someday I could be an extra on *M.A.S.H.* Maybe someday I could play Arnold's girlfriend on *Happy Days*. Maybe I could play a hooker in something." She was asked why she makes fun of her race, and she answered. "To be able to talk about race and ethnicity freely, in order to laugh and enjoy that aspect of it, is very important" (McDaniel).

Cho on Women

Ms. magazine featured Margaret Cho on the cover of its Spring 2003 issue with three other famous women (including Whoopi Goldberg) wearing a tee shirt that said, "This Is What Feminism Looks Like." The article leads with a quote by Cho: "If you say you're not a feminist you're almost denying your own existence. To be a feminist is to be alive" (58). Absurd cultural expectations for women come under fierce comic attack in a Cho concert. *I'm The One That I Want* relates how Cho's diet in preparation for her television show led to her hospitalization. As someone who struggles with a life-long eating disorder (*I'm the One That I Want*, DVD), Cho was pained by the public's negative reaction to her weight, and her negative press became a significant factor in her consequent self-destructive binge. Her book and concert detail her steady decline as she struggled through the network's punishing diet and became the butt of tabloid attacks, making fun of her "thunder thighs" and full face. Cho still manages to make this heart-rending story funny: "I didn't know I was the GIANT face taking over America." She goes on: "The sad part was that I believed it." "The first thing you lose on a diet is brain mass" (*I'm the One That I Want*, DVD).

Cho takes this theme to an even more serious level in the end of the concert when she rants against cultural complicity in making women feel badly about their bodies. In the *Ms.* article Cho states, "the tyranny of it; we're making women almost die to be beautiful" (58). In the concert, she asks over and over again how much time she would save if she stopped taking the extra second every time she saw herself in the mirror to "call myself a big fat fuck." What would happen if she stopped cringing over a photograph of herself, or stopped pulling in her gut when she passed a plate glass window? Her answer: "I save ninety-seven minutes. I can take a pottery class." She directly urges women to free themselves of the cultural brain-washing that makes them feel physically unacceptable. Of women's magazines she says, "I look at that and I think, if that is what a woman is supposed to be, then I must not be one." She directly addresses all those she sees as damaged by a dominant culture that sets strict limits of acceptance on beauty, sexual preference, and race. She includes people of intelligence and integrity as those the dominant culture has no use for. "And it is going to be really hard to find messages of self-love and support anywhere, especially in women's and gay men's culture. It's all about how you have to look . . .." Cho calls for a revolution from the dominant culture's negative messages urging conformity of appearance and behavior. She argues that self-esteem is revolutionary and a challenge to shallow norms of society.

CHO'S TECHNIQUE

How does someone this serious actually achieve popularity as a comedian? First, Cho is an actress. Her gestures, her faces, and her voices are irresistible. Cho dramatizes her stories by imitating many of her characters. A favorite personality is Cho's mother, whose strong Korean accent and constant questioning of Cho's behavior sprinkle the concerts with humanity. When Cho claimed in her first concert that she had slept with a woman, her mother, upset, phoned her: "Are you gay? Are you gay? Pick up your phone. If you don't pick up your phone that mean you're gay. Only gay screen the call" (*Notorious C.H.O.*). Another Cho technique involves sucking in her cheeks after she repeats something ridiculous and waiting for the meaning of what she has just said to permeate the audience.

In addition to physical actions, Cho uses rhythm and timing to vary the pace, add interest, and make a point. Repetition, for example, gets laughs and ensures that the audience hears the absurdity of certain remarks. In *Notorious C.H.O.*, she repeats her boyfriend's asking her why she can't come to orgasm more easily. The incessant repetition of such an intimate remark brings the audience to laughter while emphasizing the point that sexual pleasure is different for men and for women, and that men who want to be good lovers need to be patient. Cho caps off the end of some sections. For example, at the end of this section, she said her boyfriend asked her not to put this on stage. "My bad," Cho says mischievously, and moves onto the next topic.

Finally, Cho's comedy is enhanced by the structure of her shows. Each show consists of a number of random topics that appear to have no connection, but then pay off at the end. Rather than generating laughter in a vacuum, Cho builds audience laughter toward a larger issue, which is not immediately apparent. In *Notorious C.H.O.* she apparently rambles through gay life, her mother, race, sex, and weight, until she forcibly connects all the topics when she talks about those excluded from mainstream culture. She counterposes victimization and activism as ways of handling prejudice, and she urges activism. What appear to be bawdy stories haphazardly strung together actually connect the audience of outsiders to each other. As the stories build, they themselves become a cumulative force against social oppression, a statement in themselves of rebellion.

ELLEN DEGENERES

Ellen DeGeneres was born in 1958 in New Orleans, Louisiana. In an interview with Terry Gross on *Fresh Air*, she recalled how she began telling jokes and doing imitations to cheer up her mother who was suffering through a series of unsuccessful boyfriends: "…I saw the power, as a thirteen-year-old kid, to take care of my mother, to change her mood, to make her happy when she was so unhappy." When DeGeneres was twenty, she wrote a piece to help her cope with the accidental death of her lover. In this work, "A Phone Call to God," she asked God why certain things happen on earth, like fleas (DeGeneres *Fresh Air* 5). This was her first written comedy, and it catapulted her to success. Her 1982 videotaped stand-up performance from her local club won her Showtime's award for Funniest Person in America and led in 1986 to a performance on Johnny Carson's *Tonight Show*. She has appeared in several HBO's comedy specials, including *Women of the Night* (1987) and *One Night Stand: Command Performance* (1992), as well as in the Zinger film with the National Film Board of Canada's documentary on women comedians, *Wisecracks* (1991).

While she continued her stand-up, her national visibility increased, helped by her hosting the 1994 Emmy Awards telecast. Guest appearances on such shows as *Roseanne* (1995), *Mad About You* (1998), *The Larry Sanders Show* (1998), *Will and Grace* (1998), *Saturday Night Live* (2001), and *The Tonight Show with Jay Leno* reinforced her celebrity status. DeGeneres has also found success as a film actress with a variety of roles, including the voice of the fish Dory in *Finding Nemo* (2003) and of the Prologue Dog in *Doctor Doolittle* (1998). *Coneheads* (1993), *Mr. Wrong* (1996), and *EDtv* (1999) stand as some of her many movies. In 2000 DeGeneres served as executive producer and an actor in a unique HBO movie, *If These Walls Could Talk II*, which featured three stories of the lives of lesbians. The movie merited comment from comedian Kate Clinton, who said she never thought she would live long enough to see a program about the lives of lesbian women on mainstream television (*Read These Lips*). DeGeneres played Ellen Morgan in the TV show *Ellen* for five years and then followed it with a television season as Ellen Richmond in *The Ellen Show* (2001).

DeGeneres' standing in the entertainment industry is confirmed by many awards for acting and by several hosting opportunities, including several Grammy and Emmy shows. Her work hosting the 2001 Primetime Emmy's was distinguished for helping the audience cope with the events of September 11. DeGeneres also achieved fame as an author when her first book, *My Point. . . and I Do Have One* (1995) topped the *New York Times* bestseller list.[3]

In 1997 *Time* featured Ellen DeGeneres, her picture accompanied by the caption, "Yep, I'm Gay." Since DeGeneres' television character came out at the same time, the event had wide cultural significance. "The Puppy Episode," as the coming out episode was called, attracted forty-six million viewers and earned DeGeneres a Peabody Award and an Emmy for its writing. The gay community, in particular, was encouraged by the event. In an interview with Diane Sawyer on *Prime Time*, one year after the coming out episode, DeGeneres quoted from grateful letters she had received from gays, such as: "I just want to thank you again for giving me the courage to be true to myself and letting me realize that I'm not a nasty sick person." By this time ABC had decided to cancel the show due to dwindling audience response. Robert Iger, President of ABC, explained to Sawyer in the same *Prime Time* interview that the show was cancelled primarily "because of sameness. Not gayness. Sameness.... It became a program about a lead character who was gay every single week. And I just think that was too much for people." Before it cancelled the show ABC had also labeled some of the episodes with parental advisories. DeGeneres told Sawyer "It just felt so degrading.... I love someone, and because of who I choose to love, I get a warning label." Sawyer asked DeGeneres if she gave up renewal of the show in order to be a pioneer. DeGeneres answered: "Yes. If I just had this one year of doing what I did on television, I'll take that over 10 more years being on a sitcom and just being funny."

In 2002, five years after she came out, DeGeneres had a different perspective, which she shared with Marlo Thomas in the book, *The Right Words at the Right Time*. In the book Thomas gathered stories from people about key moments in their lives (79–83), and DeGeneres unfolded the background story of events which led to her coming out publicly. She revealed that although she had been out to her family since she was twenty-one, she had been afraid to come out professionally. In the first fifteen years of her career she was doing stand-up in bars where the comedians whom she followed were often mocking gays. Since a comedian has to win an audience over in the first few minutes, DeGeneres was concerned that she would alienate them if they knew she was gay. An event in 1995 changed her life course, when her manager gave her a gift of a week seminar at the Esalen Institute in California, "Changing the Dialogue of Your Inner Subconscious." The workshop led DeGeneres to the conclusion that she was living with a damaging amount of dishonesty: "My monologue was constant—don't let people know you're gay or they won't like you. Once I spoke that truth at the seminar, I couldn't live with the false version of myself anymore" (81).

DeGeneres and her manager, who had also attended the workshop, made the decision for her television character, Ellen Morgan, to come out on her television show. Their motivation was "to educate people in a creative way" (81). DeGeneres reports that while many consequences of the decision were positive, it finally resulted not only in the loss of her show, but also in some frightening personal attacks (82). DeGeneres had always feared she would be killed if she made her sexual orientation public, and she began to receive death threats. The boycott of the television show by some sponsors confirmed some of DeGeneres' worst fears (82). When she began to lose her audience, DeGeneres realized that things were out of balance, as she told Thomas: "What I did in coming out became bigger than my career, bigger than my talent, bigger than whether I'm funny or not. Everything that I had worked for over fifteen years was pushed aside and I became an unintended icon" (82).

At the time of her show the Gay & Lesbian Alliance Against Defamation sponsored a "Come Out With Ellen Day," but not all segments of society cheered at DeGeneres' decision to use television to extend tolerance toward gay life. The powerful Christian right with its adamant position that homosexuality is immoral took an activist stand against DeGeneres' show. Reverend Jerry Falwell, one of the leaders of the Christian Coalition, stated on *Larry King Live* that he had written commercial sponsors of *Ellen* and asked them to withdraw their support in the name of family values. J.C. Penney and Chrysler dropped their sponsorship, according to a *Time* report. Falwell explained in the King interview that when gay life is presented positively on television "we tempt children to experiment and go after something they normally would not." The withdrawal of sponsorship was part of a constellation of factors that led finally to the network's cancellation of the show. In countless interviews DeGeneres was asked to respond to attacks on her show, attacks on her sexual orientation, and the overwhelming publicity at the breakup of her relationship with the actress Anne Heche. The disappointments, controversies, and unending media attention affected her comedy work. Her 2000 concert and her 2003 concert are in many ways opposites and show her moving away from gay themes, thus, stepping back from her position as a gay icon, one she claims she never intended.

THE CONCERTS

Ellen DeGeneres: The Beginning (2000)

The HBO comedy special *Ellen DeGeneres: The Beginning* (2000) shows DeGeneres in a new light. Somewhat battle weary from her fights with the network and the cancellation of *The Ellen Show* and clearly beleaguered by the controversy over her coming out, Ellen DeGeneres, the comedian, searches for new footing in this show. Because of her success for seven years on television, she had not done stand-up in some time. Her decision to write this show and test it out on the road in major cities was a bold attempt to reenter the world of stand-up where she feels she belongs. Some of the first words of the concert are spoken in a cracked voice through tears: "This is a very emotional night for me. This has been quite a journey for me, to lead to this night, since I made my decision to come out three years ago" (*The Beginning*, DVD, Chapter One).

The show evinces several signs of starting over: the title, her vulnerability, a sparkling set, and riskier material. At the same time, there is very little sense of confrontation, only a sense that she would like to present herself more honestly and completely. She addresses the issue of coming out at the beginning of the show, saying that since enough has been said about it, it's better to show the audience the key points in interpretative dance. A funny sequence follows where drums start up and she mimes a shout of "I'm gay." This is followed by a frenetically upbeat dance, which ultimately dissolves into her being pulled apart in two directions and eventually sinking into a depressed crouch, burying her whole body in her arms. Lights go down, and it is not clear that she will ever get up. Finally she stands on her own two feet again and presents herself to the audience. This surprising and original introduction communicates the message that her coming out has sent her through a seismic shift and that this concert will be different. It establishes the physical sense of the whole show, announcing a new level of risk.

Gone is the innocent young Ellen who did the "A Phone Call to God" (*Women of the Night*). In this concert when she meets God, God is a beautiful middle-aged black woman. Gone is the straight-laced Ellen. She tells the story of wanting to be led to the inner light, only to realize she is out of rum. In the liquor store she purchases rum, cigarettes, and papers. Gone is the shying away from sexual material. In one comic story called "Health Food Store," she tells of being arrested while blowing up an inflatable doll from a sex shop. As she recalls in the story, she's wearing nothing but a harness, a captain's hat, and a paddle. The cop says, "You have the right to remain silent." She says, "That's all I was looking for all along." Gone is the neutral persona, replaced now by an attitude. The main character of this concert criticizes nuns and waiters, argues with meter maids and patrolmen.

While her persona is edgier, it isn't preachy or confrontational. She teases the audience on this point by saying that the world has to change and she will say the things that need to be said, "For instance, do we still need directions on the back of shampoo bottles?" (*The Beginning, DVD*). Though these "fake outs" are typical of the concert, DeGeneres does address some controversial issues. She quotes Nelson Mandela about finding the courage to be personally powerful. Addressing the subject of the religious right, she reports that some people fear that if society allows same-sex marriage, it will lead to humans' wanting to marry animals. "These people scare me, and they think we're weird. . . ." "I don't want to marry a goat. I don't even want to date one." She then imagines bringing the goat home, saying this would challenge even the most liberal parents: "Mom, dad, this is Billy." Thus, she takes the opportunity to mock the extreme ways her sexuality has been characterized.

A touching portion of the concert takes place after the show in a conversation with the audience. One young woman shows DeGeneres her college textbook, *Gender Roles*, and tells Ellen she's in it as a role model. Another person, whom DeGeneres address as "Sir," turns out to be a gay woman, who tells Ellen that she has been her role model and that DeGeneres' coming out has given her hope and promise for her own future (*Here and Now*, DVD). Although DeGeneres stated in her interview with Terry Gross that her humor had not changed, that it had always been "just basic," *The Beginning* concert shows a brasher, more sensual, and outspoken DeGeneres.

Ellen DeGeneres: Here and Now (2003)

DeGeneres' 2003 concert, *Here and Now,* pulls back from the bolder stance and controversial material of *The Beginning* concert and returns to a more mainstream and characteristic comedy. *Here and Now* hearkens back to days when life seemed simpler and Americans loved the television show *Mayberry*. DeGeneres carefully chooses topics for their universal appeal and their everyday nature. Her underlying theme is procrastination and she talks about only neutral subjects such as the news, the weather, coffee shops, and cell phones going out. She even says at one point in the concert, "I wouldn't mind hearing a few more please and thank you's." This is a far cry from the concert only three years earlier when DeGeneres joked about videotaping sex and about having sex with herself in the airplane bathroom.

In this concert, DeGeneres clearly wants to distance herself from her position as gay leader and relinquish her role as any kind of gay representative. As she said in her interview with Terry Gross, "I'm a gay person, and I certainly don't represent every gay person." She opened her concert emphasizing how many different kinds of people are in the audience, and referred to those who had to get babysitters, as if to make a special connection with families. To break the expectation that it will be a "gay" concert, she says, "We're all here . . . with all our differences, we all have one thing in common, (long pause), we're all gay." She refers to that as her one obligatory gay reference and continues by saying that the one thing that we all actually do have in common is that we all want to laugh. That is the lead line for the concert as she strikes up her theme of procrastination. She ends the concert with the line: "Procrastinate now, don't put it off!"

The physical elements of *Here and Now* also reinforce her intention to get back to basics. Replacing the flashy staging of *The Beginning*, Ellen stands before a plain curtain, plainly dressed in black pants and a navy sweater, making no attempt to call attention to her body or her sexuality. At the same time, this is a very physical concert, where she clowns out certain jokes. In an observation about how lazy we've become, she almost falls off the moving walkway at the airport. When munching popcorn at the movies, she makes silly mic sounds and serious "eating" faces. While trying to get toilet paper out of a big wheel in a public bathroom, she bends to the ground and attempts to claw out the one ply. In a very funny routine, she tries to fake out an automatic toilet flusher that won't flush by pretending to leave again.

The Norman Rockwell glow of this concert would be too much to bear, if DeGeneres were not genuinely funny. Her writing is clever and economic. She ends a routine on phones with a question of the real advantage of a cordless phone which allows us to do other things while we talk: "Chances are if you need two hands to do something, your brain should be involved in it too." She sprinkles the whole concert with the offhand remark or the surprise ending. She refers to the telephone service of call waiting as the "Mini Peoples' Choice Award," because it forces a choice of whose call to accept when two people call at the same time, assuring that one will be treated rudely. Deriding America's eating habits at movies, she mimics someone asking for popcorn in a barrel, since a bucket is not quite enough.

DeGeneres easily engages an audience, using her full smile and taking the time to enjoy their laughter and applause. She appears completely in charge, at-ease on the stage with none of the vulnerability that marked *The Beginning*. As she jockeys to find her position regarding political and feminist issues, DeGeneres assumes a non-political stance. DeGeneres the comedian primarily wants to be a writer who makes people laugh, "You know, all I ever wanted to do was, you know, be a funny person" (*Fresh Air* 4).

While the work of Ellen DeGeneres is gentler and less satirical than other women in this study, there is nevertheless an ideal in that work. One goal of the women pioneers studied here was to free women to do comedy and to free audiences to accept comedy from a woman. To a very wide audience Ellen DeGeneres unfolds a world where everyone, regardless of race, gender, or sexual preference, can enjoy the healing power of laughter. Despite some of its negative repercussions for her, DeGeneres' choice to come out so publicly was a courageous one, and one for which she has paid a price. Ironically, that choice has enriched the world of stand-up because it led her back to the stand-up stage. While DeGeneres' 2003 comedy concert communicates her desire to separate her personal life from her comedy, it also shows her successfully negotiating the rocky contours of fame. That a woman stand-up could become such a celebrity is in itself a measure of how far women in comedy have come.

Margaret Cho and Ellen DeGeneres both make significant contributions to the lengthening tradition of women in comedy. While each is remarkably talented and remarkably successful, it is unlikely that either woman could have achieved her level of success without the risks of the pioneers of comedy: Phyllis Diller, Lily Tomlin, and Roseanne. Both Cho and DeGeneres have recovered from their reportedly difficult treatment at the hands of the networks, and both have returned to their impressive careers as inventive and riveting stand-ups.

WOMEN'S STAND-UP AND MAINSTREAM TELEVISION

Challenges faced by Magaret Cho and Ellen DeGeneres come into better focus when viewed against the larger picture of the relationship of network television to the stand-up comedian and female actress. An increasingly important phenomenon for women's stand-up in the '90s was the degree to which women comedians and women stand-ups had taken a dominant position in network prime time programming. In 1993, *Time* reflected on the growing number of comedians starring in fall shows, including Thea Vidale and Brett Butler (78). Richard Zoglin, the *Time* reporter, pointed out the impact that the stand-up as star was having on the whole process of developing a sitcom: "Producers once dreamed up concepts and then looked for actors to flesh them out. Now, more often, the stars come first and the shows are built around them. It's the season of the star vehicle, the series build to a performer's specifications" (78).

Zoglin shows how the high ratings earned by *Roseanne!* and *Seinfeld* began to reshape the way networks developed sitcoms. Rather than sitting outside the development room, producers and studio executives began combing comedy clubs looking for the next talent. The success of *Home Improvement* and *Martin* with stand-ups Tim Allen and Martin Lawrence added to this phenomenon (78). At the same time, as is typical with television, there was a sense of doom hanging over the whole trend. In 1995, *Broadcasting & Cable* ran an article "Post '95 Sitcom Strength Debated," in which Steven Coe explores the possibility that there will be few if any shows to match the success of *Home Improvement* and *Seinfeld* in the syndication market (19). Nonetheless, female comedians and stand-ups continued to be hired in major roles.

In the fall of 1996, Lily Tomlin joined Candice Bergen in *Murphy Brown* as Murphy's boss, a role she would have for two years.[4] Roseanne entered her ninth season, Brett Butler continued her successful show *Grace Under Fire*, and Ellen DeGeneres starred in her show *Ellen*. Tomlin went on to play the President's assistant, Debby Fiderer, in the NBC series *The West Wing*, starring Martin Sheen. (For her role, she was nominated in 2003 for Outstanding Performance by a Female Actor in a Drama Series by the Screen Actor's Guild.) In 2000 CBS added the comedian Bette Midler to their lineup with *The Bette Show* (Carter E10). *Saturday Night Live*'s Jane Curtin won two Emmys in her role in CBS' *Kate & Allie* and went on to her role in NBC's *Third Rock From the Sun*. Julia Louis-Dreyfus, also from *Saturday Night Live*, co-starred on *Seinfeld* (Fretts 104).

Scholars of popular culture rightly questioned whether television would ultimately dilute the edgy, subversive comedy by which comedians like Roseanne initially won reputations. Does performance for mainstream television mean that feminist themes will simply be co-opted? Critic Philip Auslander offers an interesting viewpoint on this issue, stating that "mass-cultural status in and of itself does not vitiate a genre's or test's potential to do positive political work" (316). However, the final cancellation of almost all the above programs would argue that tolerance for women, even funny women, in major untraditional roles wore thin, or at least could not sustain high ratings.

These female comedians showcased a variety of women's lives, most of which, while largely white and middle class, challenged stereotypes of the "traditional woman." Even though in most cases the women did not write or produce the show (Roseanne and DeGeneres being the notable exceptions), the shows' writers featured women's experiences.

Responsibilities and competencies of women were emphasized in the role of Brett Butler as a divorced woman with children, or the roles for Tomlin and Bergen of working women, or that of a working woman, Ellen Morgan, who ran a bookstore. In *Grace Under Fire*, for example, Grace (Butler), a divorced mother, negotiated complicated family issues as she tried to raise her children. Grace attempted to maintain her children's connection and respect for their father and his parents, even though she herself disagreed with many of their values and most of their behavior. Tomlin added her skills to a show where Murphy Brown made sure that her viewpoint and talents did not get run over in the name of the patriarchal order. Tomlin's role in the sitcom added the twist of two powerful women battling for dominance. Tomlin described her character, new head of the FYI newsroom, as "a parent trying to deal with four adolescents" (qtd. in Garner 6E). In the 1996 season of *Ellen*, Ellen Morgan, backed off from her position as bookstore owner and sold the store in order to buy her own house, demonstrating another option for single women.

Pressures in the culture may work against women in untraditional roles as sitcom stars. We have already examined the effects of the religious right on the cancellation of Ellen DeGeneres' show, *Ellen*. More subtly, a cultural context not yet fully supportive of women television leads and women's themes in sitcoms was finally unable to support a lesbian lead actress. At the very least there appears to be ambivalence toward women in major sitcom roles as represented in these contrasting newspaper stories. In 1998 *The New York Times* ran an article, "Must She TV," surveying the list of upcoming shows with female themes and projecting them as a "failing line-up" (Carter B9). By contrast, a 2001 article in the same paper offered promise for shows featuring women characters, such as *The Geena Davis Show*, *Three Sisters*, and *What About Joan*. The reporter, Hilary DeVries, suggests that as more female executives gain a foothold in the television industry there will be more sitcoms created by women and featuring women. The popular form of soap opera, which plays to a largely female audience, might itself work against any trend to feature women in untraditional roles, since that genre appeals to the most traditional romantic fantasies of women.

Due to the increasing power balance between the genders, those comic actresses who do succeed in sitcoms want some consonance between their roles and their own values of equality. These values still come into major conflict with mainstream broadcasting. Deborah LeVine, creator of ABC's *Lois and Clark:*

The New Adventures of Superman, lost her job producing the show when she balked at the network's suggestion to "make Lois sweeter and give Superman more action scenes" (qtd. in Miller 16F). Women are no longer content to be the ones spoken about and not the actors. They are not interested in roles with little character development. Against these concerns, the networks find themselves under constant pressure to find successful sitcoms. *The New York Times* reported on this phenomenon in an article "No Laughing Matter for Networks: A Dearth of Successful Sitcoms," a matter which could have headlined in any year in the '90s (Rutenberg E1). However, the popularity of reality TV might diminish the importance of gender concerns in favor of those of job survival for actors.

In 2002 the Screen Actors Guild, which represents actors for movies and television, reported a 9.3 percent drop in the number of roles for SAG members from 2000 to 2001. In 2000 there were 58,134 roles as opposed to 48,167 roles in 2001. The report noted that supporting roles showed the biggest decline. The rise of reality TV was a factor cited as a partial reason for the decline in acting jobs.[5] In 2003, shows like *The Family*, *Survivor*, *Joe Millionaire*, and *The Bachelor*, riveted America's attention on its two favorite subjects, sex and money. In this television milieu gender equality takes several giant steps backwards. As a reporter for *Ms.* suggested, "Things are not good in 'Reality TV' land when you find yourself thinking the Miss America pageant is an enlightened three-hour program."

CONCLUSION: WOMEN AND COMEDY

An examination of the period from 1955 to the beginning of the twenty-first century shows enormous growth in the work of women in comedy. Phyllis Diller, who worked almost fifty years as a comic, showed great courage as she entered the arena of stand-up and moved into the mainstream when no one thought a woman could do it. Her domestic humor broke through the fortified image of "perfect mother and family," so revered in her day. Lily Tomlin's work took the journey of comedy further as she turned the path away from the conventional family life and entered the world of those on the edges of society, the homeless, the poor, single moms, and gays. Tomlin's work in Jane Wagner's play, *The Search for Signs of Intelligent Life in the Universe*, is as compassionate as it is humorous, with its biting social satire of society's clichéd solutions to complex human problems. Markedly feminist, the work focuses on the power of women in all walks of life and economic strata. Roseanne "carried the torch" for working class women so that they could see themselves as powerful. Both in her stand-up and in her long running sitcom, *Roseanne!*, she showcased working women as strong, funny survivors in a punishing system of capitalism that rarely gives blue collar workers a break, despite its idealistic promises.

From the force of the Women's Movement in the '70s and '80s, women began to stand up more. In coffee houses and on comedy stages women were finding audiences both in the mainstream and among select groups. Kate Clinton, a comedian on the lesbian circuit, gradually sharpened her satiric edge to mercilessly criticize government and religion for their institutional failures to minister to people's real needs. Paula Poundstone, also a political satirist, combined this skill with a routine about raising kids and pets. Clinton's and Poundstone's humor, with its differing audiences, begins to show the range and diversity of women comedians. Whoopi Goldberg, who with Kate Clinton and Paula Poundstone, began her career in the '80s, went from the stand-up stage and one-woman shows to a very successful career in film. Goldberg, raised in a housing project by a single mom, created a body of solo work that brought humorous attention to those disenfranchised by mainstream America. Her call for more equitable treatment of the poor, people of color, and women runs thematically through the body of her comedic work, and she has used her prominence to highlight these issues.

The work of Margaret Cho and Ellen DeGeneres shows two differing directions for stand-up today. Cho, brash, sexually explicit, and politically charged, takes her edgy comedy on the road to audiences who prefer the fringe to the mainstream. Because she is Korean-American, her comedy appeals to many in the Asian community, and she uses race as both a source of humor and of satire. Her blasts at unfair patriarchal standards attract gays, women, and those concerned with political and social justice. Ellen DeGeneres, on the other hand, works as a popular mainstream comedian by simply telling observational stories about daily life. Her stories exclude no one, because her humor focuses on the ironies and absurdities confronted by everyone. Her content is not satiric or sexually explicit, but her tenacity as a professional stand-up serves notice that an "out" woman can be one of the most successful comedians of her day.

The enormous changes experienced by women in comedy read like a social history of the United States. Phyllis Diller and Margaret Cho demonstrate a world of difference in what society will find funny. Diller's one-line jokes on domestic topics were as funny in her day as Cho's colorful stories about the shallowness of society are today. The presence, variety, and depth of women comedians manifest the growing power of women in society. Courageous in the act of standing up, they intelligently offer their viewpoint on the world and make fun of oppression in any form.

Just as the shaman in ancient society performed rituals to draw out disease and destroy it, our contemporary comedians draw out complacency and replace it with thoughtful laughter. As they generate laughter to widen cracks in the monolith of the acceptable, they empower a communal response against the absurd in our lives. Women comedians, in particular, work against the dominant order and point it toward a day when a gender equal society no longer needs comedians to laugh at its prejudices. Employing the antics of the clown rather than the sermons of the minister, these women come through the back door to affront what is off-kilter in society.

A half century view of comedy by women in solo performance makes clear that comedy's terrain occupies a much more complex territory than would first appear. As women continue to generate humor, they place themselves in a powerfully creative position. As William Fry, Professor Emeritus of Psychiatry at Stanford University, states: "Creativity and humor are identical. They both involve bringing two items which do not have an obvious connection and creating a relationship" (qtd. in Doskoch 1G). When interviewed for *Wisecracks*, the film on female comedians, many of the comedians marveled at the power they felt when they were in sync with the audience. The comedians, when sparked by the audience, described an exhilaration, rare in life, as Sandra Shamus described it: "You have two circles. This is the audience and this is the performer. And when they mesh, in that little space, it's the sweet spot, you're standing like a lightning rod for creativity" (qtd. in *Wisecracks*).

Skillful and aware, these women unleash their art to reshape society. Phyllis Diller pitted her own talent against a male-dominated stage and used the force of that talent to make room for herself and those who would follow her. Lily Tomlin and Jane Wagner harnessed their combined genius to create an unforgettable repertoire of characters from those who would normally not merit a second glance. Likewise, Roseanne Barr misbehaved outrageously until she had developed a disciplined and effective routine demanding dignity for the housewife and a sitcom that elevated the working class by its fierce honesty.

As Elayne Boosler pointed out, "The best who stand-up, stand-up for something."[6] Based on the evidence of this study, Lily Tomlin, Roseanne, Kate Clinton, Paula Poundstone, Whoopi Goldberg, and Margaret Cho view themselves as cultural subversives. Ellen DeGeneres is viewed by many as a cultural subversive, because she has the courage, as an openly gay woman, to be a popular comedian. Humor is not just a profession; it's a philosophy, a point of view. As these women steer their careers, the force of humor steers them. As Kate Clinton suggests, "Humor leads the way; it moves us past those inbred, ingrained resistances. We make light. We see where to go and we are light enough to move there."[7] Feminist comedians use the physical force of laughter to change the world.

Notes

NOTES TO CHAPTER ONE

[1] See Tomlin's website at <http://lilytomlin.com>

NOTES TO CHAPTER TWO

[1] See Regina Barreca's *The Penguin Book of Women's Humor* (1996), which collects memorable quotations from scores of women humorists and comedians.

NOTES TO CHAPTER FOUR

[1] Biographical information on Roseanne is plentiful, including an interactive website, <http://roseanneworld.com>, but I recommend reading her two books (Arnold, *My Lives* and Barr, *My Life As a Woman*) as the best source of significant information.

NOTES TO CHAPTER SIX

[1] See Regina Barreca, *The Penguin Book of Women's Humor*, 147.
[2] See <http://www.speaktruth.com/vaidurvashi>.
[3] See Kate Clinton's website at <http://www.kateclinton.com/bio.htm>.
[4] See Clinton website.
[5] See biography for Paula Poundstone from Richard De La Font Agency, Inc. at <http://www.delafont.com/comedians.Paula-Poundstone.htm>.
[6] See Poundstone biography from *Mother Jones* at <http://www.motherjones.com>.
[7] See Poundstone, Richard De La Font Agency, Inc.
[8] See Maynard in *Daily Variety*, Feb. 2002.

[9] See Goldberg, *Current Biography 1985*, *The Choices We Made*, ed. Angela Bonovoglia, and <http://us.imdb.com/Goldberg, Whoopi>.

[10] See Whoopi Goldberg at <http://us.imdb.com/Goldberg, Whoopi>.

[11] See Maynard, *Daily Variety*, Feb. 2002.

[12] See *Jet*, Feb. 24, 2003.

[13] See Defaa, *Entertainment Weekly*.

[14] See Cain, *Black Issues Review*.

[15] See Whoopi Goldberg at <http://us.imdb.com/Goldberg, Whoopi>.

NOTES TO CHAPTER SEVEN

[1] See section at end of this chapter on "Women's Stand-Up and Mainstream Television."

[2] See Amnesty International web site at <http://www.amnestyusa.org.

[3] See DeGeneres biographical information in the 1996 Current Biography Yearbook and web sites <http://www.ellen.warnerbros.com/bio.html> and <http://us.imbd.com/degeneres+ellen>.

[4] See Tomlin bio and web page at <http://lilytomlin.com>.

[5] See "Guild Report: Actor's Jobs Declining," *Entertainment Weekly*.

[6] See Regina Barreca, *Penguin Book of Women's Humor*, 73.

[7] See Barreca, *Penguin Book*, 147.

Bibliography

Allen, Steve. *Funny People*. New York: Stein and Day, 1981.
"Amnesty International to Honor Ellen DeGeneres." 9 Jan. 2000. <http://www.amnestyusa.org>.
Apte, Mahavdev. *Humor and Laughter: An Anthropological Approach*. Ithaca: Cornell University Press, 1985.
Aristotle. *The Poetics. The Reader's Encyclopedia of World Drama*. Ed. by John Gassner and Edward Quinn. New York: Thomas Y. Crowell Company, 1969: 937–950.
---. *The Nichomachian Ethics. The Philosophy of Laughter and Humor*. Ed. John Morreall. Albany: State University of New York Press, 1987: 14–16.
Arnold, Roseanne. *My Lives*. New York: Ballantine Books, 1994.
Auslander, Philip. "'Brought to You by Fem Rage': Stand-up Comedy and the Politics of Gender." *Acting Out: Feminist Performances*, Ed. Lynda Hart. 1993: 315–336.
Barnes, Clive. "Bang Those Tom-Toms For Tomlin." Rev. of *The Search for Signs of Intelligent Life in the Universe*. The Plymouth Theatre, New York. *New York Post*. 27 Sept. 1985. Rpt. in *The New York Times Critic Reviews*. Eds. Betty Blake and Joan Marlowe. New York: Critics' Theatre Reviews, 1985:198.
---. "Stage: 'Lily Captures Broadway.'" Rev. of *Appearing Nitely!* The Biltmore Theater, New York. *The New York Times*. 25 March 1977. Rpt. in *The New York Times Theater Reviews*. 1977. New York: *The New York Times*.
Barr, Roseanne. Agent's Biography. Marleah Leslie & Associates, Beverly Hills, Ca., March 1996.
Barr, Roseanne. Biography, <http://roseanneworld.com>.
Barr, Roseanne. *Celebrity Bios* n. pag. Lexus Nexus. 21 Sept. 1994.
Barr, Roseanne. Interview with Alan King. *Alan King: Inside the Comic Mind*.
---. *Roseanne: My Life as a Woman*. New York: Harper and Row, 1989.

Barreca, Regina, ed. and Introduction. *Last Laughs: Perspectives on Women and Comedy*. New York: Gordon and Breach, 1988.

---. ed. *New Perspectives on Women and Comedy*. Philadelphia: Gordon and Breach, 1992.

---. ed. *The Penguin Book of Women's Humor*. New York: Penguin Books, 1996.

---. *They Used to Call Me Snow White ... But I Drifted: Women's Strategic Use of Humor*. New York: Viking Press, 1991.

Beaufort, John. Rev. of *The Search for Signs of Intelligent Life in the Universe*. The Plymouth Theatre. New York. *The Christian Science Monitor*. 2 Oct. 1985. Rpt. in *New York Times Critic Reviews*. Eds. Betty Blake and Joan Marlowe. New York: Critics' Theatre Reviews, 1985:199.

Berger, Phil. *The Last Laugh*. New York: Limelight Editions, 1985.

Bergson, Henri. "Laughter." *Comedy*. Ed. Wylie Sypher. Baltimore: The Johns Hopkins University Press, 1956.

The Best of "On Location" Part One. Perf. Phyllis Diller and Bob Hope. "Bob Hope's Overseas Christmas: Around the World." Videocassette. NBC, 1980.

Blau, Joel. *The Visible Poor*. New York: Oxford University Press, 1992.

Bono, Chastity and Jerry Falwell. Interview with Larry King. "A Debate Over Ellen DeGeneres' Announcement That She is Gay." *Larry King Live*. CNN, 8 April 1997. <http://www.galegroup.com>. Transcript # 97040800V22.

Brockett, Oscar G. *History of the Theatre*. 5th ed. Boston: Allyn and Bacon, Inc., 1986.

Bruce, Lenny. *How to Talk Dirty and Influence People*. Chicago: Playboy Press, 1963.

Bruere, Martha Bensley and Mary Ritter Beard. "Laughing Their Way: Women's Humor in America." Ed. Morris. 17–21.

Burns, George. Interview. *Dateline NBC*. Jan. 1996.

Byrne, Bridget. "Arsenio Out. Roseanne Back?!" *Eonline*. 3 Apr. 1997. <http://www.galegroup.com>.

Cain, Joy Duckett. Rev. of *Book* by Whoopi Goldberg. *Black Issues Book Review*. May–June 2003: 38. <http://www.galegroup.com>.

Carter, Bill. "CBS Adds Comedies, Aiming Midler at 'Millionaire.'" *The New York Times*. 18 May 2000: p. B10. <http://www.galegroup.com>.

Carter, Bill. "Must She TV." *The New York Times*. 18 Mar 1998: E7. <http://www.galegroup.com>.

Case, Sue Ellen. *Feminism and Theatre*. New York: Methuen,1988.

Cho, Margaret. Biography. <http://us.imdb.com/bio/Cho/Margaret>.

---. *I'm the One That I Want*, filmed in live concert. DVD. 2000 Distributed by Windstar TV and video.

---. *I'm the One That I Want*. New York: Ballantine Books, 2001.

---. *Notorious C.H.O.* filmed live at Carnegie Hall. DVD. 2002.

Bibliography

Chopin, Kate. *The Awakening.* New York: Bantam (1899), 1981.
Clinton, Kate. "As Long As It Takes." *Progressive.* May 2003.
---. "Being John Ashcroft." *The Advocate.* March 2001.
---. Biography. <http.//www.kateclinton.com/bio.htm>.
---. Biography. <http://www.speak-truth.com/bio/clinton_kate.html>.
---. *Don't Get Me Started.* New York: Ballantine Books, 1998.
---. "Emergency Preparedness." *The Advocate.* May 2003.
---. *Girlfriend's Magazine.*<http://www.glbtq.com/arts/clinton>.
---. Interview with Andrea L.T. Peterson. *Camp Rehoboth.* 22 May 1998.
---. *"Making Light: Some Notes on Feminist Humor,"* unpublished essay.
---. perf. Paramount Theatre. Denver. 27 Jan.1995.
---. "Secrets of the Ha-Ha Sisterhood." *The Village Voice.* 26 June 2002. <http:www.villagevoice.com/issues/0226/clinton.php>.
Coe, Steve. "Post-'95 Sitcom Strength Debated." *Broadcasting & Cable.* 24 April 1995: 19. <http://www.galegroup.com>.
Collier, Denise, and Kathleen Beckett. *Spare Ribs: Women in the Humor Biz.* New York: St. Martin's Press, 1980.
"Comedian Phyllis Diller Ends Long Stand Up Career." *San Francisco Chronicle.* 14 Apr. 2002. <http://www.sfgate.com/new/archive/diller>.
Comic Relief. Videocassette. HBO. 1986.
Comic Relief III. Videocassette. HBO. 1989.
"A Conversation With Kate Clinton." Interview. *Womankind.* 1998. <http://www.womankindflp.org/newsletter/interviews/clinton.htm>.
Corn, David. "The Whoopi Goldberg Show." *The Nation.* 21 Dec. 1992: 775. <http:galegroup.com>.
Coser, Ruth Laub. "Laughter Among Colleagues: A Study of the Social Function of Humor Among the Staff of a Mental Hospital." *Psychiatry.* Feb. 1960: 81–95.
Current Biography 1967. New York: The H. H. Wilson Company, 1967.
Defaa, Chip. "That Thing She Does." *Entertainment Weekly.* 14 Feb.1999. <http://www.galegroup.com. Article 19098061>.
DeGeneres, Ellen. 1996 *Current Biography Yearbook.*
---. *Ellen DeGeneres: The Beginning.* DVD. HBO, 2000
---. *Ellen DeGeneres: Here and Now.* HBO, 28 June, 2003.
---. Filmography. <http://us.imdb.com/degeneres,+ellen>.
---. Interview with Terry Gross. *Fresh Air.* National Public Radio. WHYY. Philadelphia. 23 May 2003. (previously broadcast in 2002) Transcript by Burrelle's Information Service, Livingston, N.J.
---. My bio, pics, & video. <http.//ellen.warnerbros.com/bio.html.>.
---. *My Point…and I Do Have One.* New York: Bantam Books, 1995.
---. and Iger, Robert. Interview with Diane Sawyer. "Ellen Uncensored: Views On Why Her Show Was Cancelled." *Prime Time.* ABC. New York. 6 May 1998.

DeMause, Lloyd. *Reagan's America*. New York: Creative Roots, Inc. Publishers, 1984.

De Vries, Hilary. "In Comedies, Signs of a New Women's Movement; as Female TV Executives Gain More Power." *The New York Times*. 25 Feb. 2001:19. <http//:galegroup.com>.

Diamond, Elin. "Mimesis, Mimicry, and the True-Real.'" Ed. Hart 363–382.

Diller, Phyllis. *Are You Ready For Phyllis Diller?* LP. Verve. v-15031. n.d.

---. *The Best of Phyllis Diller*. LP. Verve. 15053. n.d.

---. *Born To Sing*. LP. Columbia. CS 9523. n.d.

---. *Phyllis Diller Laughs*. LP. Verve. V6-15026. n.d.

---. Telephone Interview. 20 March 1996.

---. *What's Left of Phyllis Diller*. LP. Verve. V-15059. n.d.

---. Biography. <http://www.delafon.com/comedians/E/phyllisdiller.htm>.

---. *Contemporary Authors Online*. Gale, 2003. Reproduced in *Biography Resource Center*. Farmington Hill, Mich.: The Gale Group. 2003. <http://www.galegroup.com>.

---. *Current Biography 1967*. The W. H. Wilson Company, 1967.

---. Interview with Harriet Barovick. "Risky Business: How a Book Helped a Housewife Jump-Start a Pioneering Career As a Comic." *Time*. 18 June 2001.

---. *St. James Encyclopedia of Popular Culture*. 5 vols. St. James Press, 2000. Reproduced in *Biography Resource Center*. Farmington Hill, Mich.: The Gale Group. 2003. <http://www.galegroup.com>.

---. and Jim Nabors, perf. Harrah's Casino, South Lake Tahoe, California. 21 Sept. 1996.

Dimeglio, John E. *Vaudeville U.S.A.* Ohio: Bowling Green University Popular Press, 1973.

Doskoch, Peter. "Humor Me." *The Denver Post*. 9 Oct. 1996: 1G.

Draper, Ruth. *The Art of Ruth Draper*. Audiocassette. Spoken Arts, 1983.

Dresner, Zita Z. "Whoopi Goldberg and Lily Tomlin: Black and White Women's Humor." *Women's Comic Visions*. Ed. June Sochen. Detroit: Wayne State University Press, 1991.

Dumas, Alan. "Topical Solutions: Paula Poundstone's foster children bring domesticity into the focus of her wit." *Rocky Mountain News*. 8 May 1996: Spotlight 9D.

Dusky, Lorraine. "*Ms*. Poll: Feminist Tide Sweeps in As the 21st Century Begins." *Ms*. Spring 2003: Cover plus 56+.

Dworkin, Susan. "Roseanne Barr: The Disgruntled Housewife as Standup Comedian." *Ms*. July/August 1987: 106-108, 205-6.

Farmighetti, Robert, ed. *The World Almanac and Book of Facts 1995*. New York: Funk and Wagnalls Corporation. 1994.

Fink, Jerry. "Family Woman." *Las Vegas Sun*. 3 Feb. 2001. <http://galegroup.com>.

Bibliography

Fisher, Seymour and Rhoda Fisher. *Pretend the World is Funny and Forever: A Psychological Analysis of Comedians, Clowns and Actors.* New Jersey: Lawrence Erlbaum Associates, 1981.

Fretts, Bruce. "Remote Patrol." *Entertainment Weekly.* 27 June 1997: 104-5. <http//: galegroup.com>.

Friedan, Betty. *The Feminine Mystique.* New York: Dell, 1963.

French, Marilyn. "Lily Tomlin." *Ms.* Jan. 1986: 32-34.

Freud, Sigmund. *Jokes and Their Relation To The Unconscious.* New York: W. W. Norton and Company, 1963.

Frutkin, Alan. "Television's 23 Gay Characters." *The Advocate.* 18 Feb. 1997: 30.

Funny Women of Television. Forty Years of Television. Dir. Louis Horovitz. Videocassette. NBC, Oct. 1991.

Gagnier, Regenia. "Between Women: a cross-class analysis of status and anarchic humor." *Last Laughs.* Ed. Barreca 135-147.

Garner, Jack. "Murphy's New Boss." *The Denver Post.* 26 Sept. 1996: 8E.

Gassner, John, and Edward Quinn, eds. *The Reader's Encyclopedia of World Drama.* New York: Thomas Y. Crowell Company, 1969.

"Goldberg and Gregory Feted at Comedy Festival." *Jet.* 25 March 2002:1 <http://www.us.imdb.com/goldberg/whoopi>.

"Goldberg, Whoopi: Awards, Biography, and Filmography." http://www.us.imdb.com/goldberg/whoopi.

Goldberg, Whoopi. *Book.* New York: William Morrow and Company, Inc., 1997.

---. *Chez Whoopi.* Dir. Prod. Rocco Urbisci. Videocassette. HBO, 1991.

---. *Current Biography Yearbook 1985.* New York: The H.W. Wilson Company: 1985.

---. Ed. Angela Bonavoglia. *The Choices We Made: 25 Men and Women Speak Out About Abortion.* New York: Random House, 1991.

---. "Goldberg's Prepared for Fourth Fling." Interview with Kevin Maynard. *Variety.* 4 Mar. 2002:55 <http://www.galegroup.com>.

Graham, Marilyn F. and Beverly Birns. "Where Are The Women Geniuses? Up the Down Escalator." Ed. Kopp 291-312.

The Great Standups. Sixty Years of Laughter. A Tug of Duck Production. Videocassette. HBO, 1985.

Gross, Brenda. "The Parallel Lives of Kathy and Mo." *New Perspectives on Women and Comedy.* Ed. Barreca 89-99.

"The Guild Report: Actor's Jobs Declining." *Entertainment-AP.* 3 July 2002:n.pag. <http://asian.news.yahoo.com>.

Hadas, Moses, trans. *The Complete Plays of Aristophanes.* Toronto: Bantam, 1962.

Handy, Bruce. "Roll Over, Ward Cleaver." *Time.* 14 April 1997.

Hart, Lynda, and Peggy Phelan, eds. *Acting Out: Feminist Performances.* Ann Arbor: The University of Michigan Press, 1993.

---. Introduction. *Acting Out: Feminist Performances.* Ed. Hart and Phelan 1-12.

Haig, Robin Andrew. *The Anatomy of Humor*. Springfield: Charles C. Thomas, 1988.

Henry III, William A. "Let a Hundred Lilys Bloom." Rev. of *The Search for Signs of Intelligent Life in the Universe*, by Jane Wagner. The Plymouth Theatre, New York. *Time* 7 Oct. 1985. Rpt. in *New York Times Critic Reviews*. Eds. Betty Blake and Joan Marlowe. New York: Critics' Theatre Reviews, 1985. 201.

Hymowitz, Carol, and Michaele Weissman. *A History of Women in America*. Toronto: Bantam Books, 1978.

"Interview With Kate Clinton." *SGS* 12 Oct. 2001. <http://bookish.rog/clips/Kate.htm>.

Jack Benny's Bag. Dir. Norman Abbott. Videocassette. NBC, 1968.

James, William. *Some Problems of Philosophy*. Cambridge, MA: Harvard University Press, 1979.

Johnson, Brian D. Rev. of *Wisecracks*, dir. Singer. *McClean's* 9 Sept.1991: 44. <http://www.galegroup.com. Article A11238448>.

Judge, Diane. "Talking with Lily Tomlin," *Redbook*. 16 Jan. 1981: 16.

Jung, Carl G., ed. *Man and his Symbols*. New York: Doubleday & Company Inc.,1964.

Kanfer, Stefan. "Sauce, Satire and Shtick." *Time*. Fall 1990 v 136:62+. <http://www.galegroup.com>.

Kaplan, E. Ann. *Women and Film*. New York: Methuen, 1981.

Kate Clinton. perf. Paramount Theatre, Denver. 27 Jan. 1996.

Kate Clinton: Read These Lips. CD of live concert. Uproar Entertainment. Herbst Theatre, San Francisco, CA. 21 Oct. 2000.

Kelleher, Terry. "Tube." *People Weekly*. 18 Aug. 2002:27.

Kelly, Patrick. "Margaret Cho." *2000 Current Biography Yearbook*.

Kendt, Rob. "The Wicked Stage and the Gag Reel." *Back Stage West*. 29 May 2003:11.

"Kennedy Center Honors Lily Tomlin." Lily Tomlin's official website. <http:/www.lilytomlin.com/press/kennedy-pr.htm>.

Kerr, Walter. "A Pushover for Actresses? Not me, But. . ." Rev. of *Appearing Nitely!* Biltmore Theatre, New York. *New York Times* 3 April 1977: 63-64.

Kightlinger, Laura. "Returning the Favor." *New Perspectives on Women and Comedy*. Ed. Barreca 85-88.

Koestler, Arthur. *The Act of Creation*. New York: Dell Publishing Co., Inc., 1964.

Kopp, Claire B., ed. *Becoming Female: Perspectives on Development*. New York: Plenium Press, 1979.

Koziski Olson, Stephanie. "Standup Comedy." *Humor in America*. Ed. Lawrence Mintz. N.Y.: Greenwood Press, 1988. 109-136.

Kroll, Jack. "Divinely Human Comedy." Rev. of *Search for Signs of Intelligent Life in the Universe*. Plymouth Theatre, New York. *Newsweek* 23 Sept. 1985: 200. Rpt. in *New York Times Critic Reviews*. Eds. Betty Blake and Joan Marlowe. New York: Critics' Theatre Reviews, 1985: 199.

Lahr, John. "Dealing with Roseanne." *The New Yorker*. 17 July 1995: 42–61.

Lauren, Jamie. "It's Cho Time." *No Ho LA*. 20 June 2002.

Lavin, Cheryl. "Tomlin-Wagner: match made in show-biz heaven." *The Denver Post*. 13 Nov. 1994: E2.

Lester, Stanley. "Lily Tomlin: Appearing Nitely." Rev. of *Appearing Nitely!* Biltmore Theatre, New York. *Stereo Review*. Jan. 1978: 120.

Levine, Suzanne and Harriet Lyons, eds. *The Decade of Women: A Ms. History of the Seventies in Words and Pictures*. New York: Putnam, 1980.

Lipton, Michael A. "Comic's Relief." *People Weekly*. 23 Dec 2002: 77. <http:/www.galegroup.com>.

Luehring, Donnie. "Kate Clinton." *Out Front*. 25 Jan. 1995: 11.

Mabley, Moms, perf. *Moms Mabley On Stage*. Audiocassette. Tivoli Theatre, Chicago. MCA Records, Inc., 1984.

Manchester, William. *The Glory and the Dream: A Narrative History of America, 1932–1972*. New York: Bantam Books, 1984.

Mansfield, Stephanie. "I'm So Normal: Roseanne's Not Kidding." *USA Weekend*. 13–15 Sept. 1996:4–6.

Markarius, L. "Ritual Clowns and Symbolic Behavior." *Diogenes*. 1970: 44–73.

Martin, Linda, and Kerry Segrave. *Women in Comedy*. New Jersey: Citadel Press, 1986.

Maynard, Kevin. "Goldberg Joins Peers Williams, Crystal With AFI Laurel." *Daily Variety*. 26 Feb. 2002:A4. <http://www.galegroup.com>.

McDaniel, Mike. "Margaret Cho: Notorious and Loving It." *Houston Chronicle*. 9 Jan. 2002. <http:/www.margaretcho.net/articles>.

McPhee, Paul E. "The Role of Laughter and Humor in Growing Up Female." Ed. Kopp 183–206.

Mile, Sian. "Roseanne Barr: Canned Laughter-Containing the Subject." *New Perspectives on Women and Comedy*. 1992: 39–46.

Miller, Ron. "Power Illusory in Women's TV Presence." *The Denver Post*. December, 1994:16F.

Mintz, Lawrence, ed. *Humor in America*. New York: Greenwood Press, 1988.

---. "Standup Comedy As Social and Cultural Mediation." *American Quarterly* 37:1 (Spring 1985): 71–80.

---. "The 'New Wave' of Standup Comedians: An Introduction." *American Humor: An Interdisciplinary Newsletter,* ed. T. Inge and L. E. Mintz. IV. 2. (Fall 1977): 1–3.

Merrill, Lisa. "Feminist Humor: Rebellious and Self-Affirming." *Last Laughs*. Ed. Barreca 273–278.

Morreall, John, ed. *The Philosophy of Laughter and Humor*. Albany: State University of New York Press, 1987.

Morris, Linda, ed. *American Women Humorists*. New York: Garland Publishing, Inc. 1994.

Ms. Magazine Online. <http://www.msmagazine.com/>.

Nichols, Mike and Elaine May. *The Best Of Mike Nichols and Elaine May*. LP. SR60997. Mercury Records, n.d.

---. *An Evening With Mike Nichols and Elaine May*. LP. Mercury OCM 2200. Mercury Records, n.d.

---. *Improvisations to Music*. LP. Mercury SR 60040. Mercury Records, n.d.

Norton, Mary Beth, et al., eds. *A People and a Nation*. 2nd ed. Boston: Houghton Mifflin Company, 1986.

Norwood, Gilbert. *Greek Comedy*. New York: Hill and Wang, 1963.

"A Paula Poundstone Biography." <http://www.motherjones.com/paula/bio>.

Paula Poundstone. Interview. *Entertainment Tonight*. 18 Feb 2002, <http://www.etonline.com>.

"Perspectives." *Newsweek*. 30 Sept. 1996: 27.

"Poundstone, Paula." Biography. Richard De La Font Agency, Inc. <http://www.delafont/comedians/Paula-Poundstone.htm>.

Poundstone, Paula. "He Didn't Even Like Girls." *Mother Jones*. May-June 1993: 80. <http://www.motherjones.com>.

---. "Keeping My Mouth Shut." *Mother Jones*. Jan.-Feb. 1994: 80. <http://www.motherjones.com>.

---. "National Heartthrob." *Mother Jones*. March-April 1995: 80. <http://www.motherjones.com>.

---. perf. *An Evening With Paula Poundstone*. Denver Paramount Theatre. 29 April 1995.

---. perf. Denver: Denver Auditorium Theatre. 10 May 1996.

---. "Republican Field Guide." *Mother Jones*. May-June 1995: 80. <http://www.motherjones.com>.

Perell, Robin. "Classic Kate Clinton." *X-Tra.Ca*. 31 Oct.2002. <http://www.xtra.ca/site/toronto2/archvx/body 51.shtm>.

Pershing, Linda. "There's a Joker in the Menstrual Hut: A Performance Analysis of Comedian Kate Clinton." *American Women Humorists*. Ed. Morris 383-429.

Pickard-Cambridge, Sir Arthur. *The Dramatic Festival of Athens*. Oxford: The Clarendon Press, 1968.

Pryor, Richard. *Pryor Convictions*. New York: Pantheon Books, 1995.

Reich, Robert B. *Tales of a New America*. New York: Random House, Times Books, 1987.

Rev. of *Beyond Tara: The Extraordinary Life of Hattie McDaniel*. *Jet*. 23 July 2001:20. <http://www.galegroup.com>.

Rev. of *Unchained Memories, Readings From the Slave Narratives*. HBO, 2003. narr. Whoopi Goldberg. *Jet*. 24 Feb. 2003: 54. <http://www.galegroup.com>.

Rich, Frank. Rev. of *Search for Signs of Intelligent Life in the Universe*. The Plymouth Theatre, New York. *The New York Times*. 27 Sept. 1985: C3:1.

---. "At Its Best, the Theatre Illuminated Our World." Rev. of the 1985–1986 Annual Tony Awards. *New York Times*. 30 May 1986: 157.

Robinson, Jill. "A Bunch of Lily Tomlin." *Vogue*. June 1977:148, 186–7.

Rodney Dangerfield: It's Not Easy Being Me. Prod. Paper Clip Productions, Inc. Videocassette. Orion Home Video, 1986.

Roseanne Barr. Dir. Tom Werts. Videocassete. HBO, 1991.

The Roseanne Barr Show. Prod. and Dir. Rocco Urbisci. Videocassette. HBO, 1987.

Roseanne: Live From Trump Tower. Prod. David Yarnell. Dir. Roseanne Arnold and Louis J. Horovitz. Videocassette. HBO, 1993.

Rutenberg, Jim. "No Laughing Matter for Networks: A Dearth of Successful Sitcoms." *The New York Times*. 12 May 2003: E1.

Ryan, Joal. "Roseanne Gets More Real." *Eonline*. 18 Oct. 2002.

Sager, Mike. "I've Learned: Roseanne." *Esquire*. Mar 2001: 164. <http://www.galegroup.com>.

Samuels, Allison. "Ready For Her Close-Up (Again): Hasta La Vista Hollywood. The Ineffable Whoopi Comes Back to Broadway." *Newsweek*. 10 Feb. 2003: 65+ <http://www.galegroup.com>.

Schaller, Michael. *Reckoning with Reagan*. New York: Oxford University Press, 1992.

Schindehette, Susan. "Roseanne Pitches Apologies after Throwing Fans a Curve with a Barr-Mangled Banner." *People Weekly*. 13 Aug 1990: 44. <http://www.galegroup.com>.

Shakespeare, William. *Twelfth Night. The Handy Volume Shakespeare Vol. III*. London: Bradbury, Evans and Co., 1866.

---. *King Lear. The Handy Volume Shakespeare Vol. XII*. London: Bradbury, Evans and Co., 1866.

Sheppard, Alice. "From Kate Sanborn to Feminist Psychology: The Social Context of Women's Humor, 1885–1985." Ed. Morris 109–130.

Slansky, Paul. *The Clothes Have No Emperor*. New York: Simon and Schuster, 1989.

Slide, Anthony. *The Encyclopedia of Vaudeville*. Connecticut: Greenwood Press, 1994.

Sochen, June. *Women's Comic Visions*. Detroit: Wayne State University Press, 1991.

Standing Up for Women: The Art of the Female Monologuist. Prod. Museum of Radio and Television. Videocassette. (Seminar guests: Phyllis Diller, Mo Gafney, Kathy Ladman, Carol Leifer, and Anne Meara). New York, New York. 8 June 1993.

Stoddard, Karen. "Women Have No Sense of Humor and Other Myths." *American Humor*. IV. 2. (Fall 1977): 11-14.

Stone, Elizabeth. "Understanding Lily Tomlin." *Psychology Today*. July 1977, 14+.

"Suggestions?" *Ms. Magazine Online*. <http://www.msmagazine.com>

Thomas, Bob. "Housewife-Turned-Comic Phyllis Diller Ending 47 Years of Daffy Delivery." *The Detroit News*. 6 May, 2002. <http://www.gale-group.com>.

Thomas, Evan. "The War Over Gay Marriage." *Newsweek*. 7 July 2003: 38-45.

Thomas, Marlo, ed. *The Right Words at the Right Time*. New York: Atria Books, 2002: 79-83.

Tomlin, Lily. *And That's the Truth*. LP. Polydor, PD 5023, 1972.

---. *Appearing Nitely!* Prod. Tomlin and Wagner Theatricalz. Videocassette of 1986 Los Angeles Production. Wolfe Video, 1992.

---. Awards. <http://us.imdb.com/awards/Tomlin+Lily>.

---. *Biography*. <http://lilytomlin.com/bio>.

---. *Celebrity Bios*. (17 May 1994): n.p. Lexus Nexus. 21 Sept. 1994.

---. *Ernestine: Peak Experiences*. Prod. Tomlin and Wagner Theatricalz. Videocasette of *Laugh In*, 1969, *Saturday Night Live*, 1976, and Tomlin's *Flashdance* parody. Wolfe Video, 1992.

---. *Laugh-In Reprise '69*. LP. Reprise RS 6335, 1969.

---. *Lily For President*. Prod. Tomlin and Wagner Theatricalz. Videocassette of 1982 television special. Wolfe Video, 1992.

---. *Lily Sold Out*. Prod. Tomlin and Wagner Theatricalz. Videocassette of 1981 television special. Wolfe Video, 1992.

---. *Lily Tomlin*. by Nicholas Broomfield and Joan Churchill. Prod. Pauline Canny. Videocassette. HBO, 1986.

---. *Modern Scream*. LP. Polydor. PD 6051, 1974.

---. perf. *The Search for Signs of Intelligent Life in the Universe*. by Jane Wagner. Dir. Jane Wagner. Auditorium Theatre, Denver. Oct. 1989.

---. Rev. of *The Search for Signs of Intelligent Life in the Universe*. Charles Isherwood Theatre. *Variety*. 20 Nov. 2000: 24. <http://www.galegroup.com>.

---. *The Search for Signs of Intelligent Life in the Universe*. Prod. Tomlin and Wagner Theatricalz. Videocasette. HBO 1992.

---. *This Is a Recording*. LP. Polydor, PD 244055, 1971.

Toth, Emily. "A Laughter of Their Own: Women's Humor in the United States." Ed. Morris 85-107.

Toto, Christian. "Poundstone Rests Her Case With Audience." *Washington Times*. 1 Apr 2002. <http://www.galegroup.com>.

Towsen, John H. *Clowns*. New York: Hawthorn Book, Inc, 1976.

Trager, James. *The Women's Chronology*. New York: Henry Holt and Company, 1994.

Tucker, Ken. "No Holds Barr-ed." *Entertainment Weekly*. 15 May 2000: 58.

Tynan, Kenneth. Foreward. *How to Talk Dirty and Influence People*. By Lenny Bruce. Chicago: Playboy Press, 1963. ix-sxii.

Unterbrink, Mary. *Funny Women: American Comediennes. 1860-1985*. New York: McFarland & Co., 1987.
"Vaid, Urvashi." *Speak Truth.com*. <http://www.speak-truth.com/bio/vaidurvashi.html>.
The View. ABC, 13 August 2003.
Wagner, Jane. *The Search for Signs of Intelligent Life in the Universe*. New York: Harper and Row, 1987.
Walker, Nancy. *A Very Serious Thing: Women's Humor and American Culture*. Minneapolis: University of Minnesota Press, 1988.
---. and Zita Dresner. "Redressing the Balance: American Women's Literary Humor from Colonial Times to the 1980s." Ed. Morris 33-57.
Watt, Douglas. "A darling Lily in a barren field." Rev. of *The Search for Signs of Intelligent Life in the Universe*. Dir. Jane Wagner. Plymouth Theatre. New York. Rpt. in *New York Times Critic Reviews*. Eds. Betty Blake and Joan Marlowe. New York: Critics' Theatre Reviews, Sept. 1985: 197.
Weisstein, Naomi. "Why We Aren't Laughing . . . Any More." *American Women Humorists*. Ed. Morris 131-139.
Wheeler, Carol. "Margaret Cho." *Ms*. Spring 2003: 58
---. "Whoopi Goldberg." *Ms*. Spring 2003: 59.
Who Makes You Laugh? Prod. Ernest Chambers. ABC Special. 6 May 1995.
"Whoopi Goldberg to Leave Hollywood Squares at the End of This Season." *Jet*. 6 May 2002: 20 <http://www.galegroup.com>.
Wilde, Larry. *The Great Comedians Talk About Comedy*. New York: The Citadel Press, 1968.
---. *How the Great Comedy Writers Create Laughter*. Chicago: Nelson-Hall, 1976.
Winer, Linda. "Lily Tomlin's 'Search' finds brilliant life." Rev. of *The Search for Signs of Intelligent Life in the Universe*. The Plymouth Theatre, New York. *USA Today* 27 Sept. 1985. Rpt. in *New York Times Critic Reviews*. Eds. Betty Blake and Joan Marlowe. New York: Critics' Theatre Reviews, 1985. 198.
Wisecracks. A Zinger film production in co-production with The National Film Board of Canada. Videocassette. Monarch Home Video. 1993.
Women of the Night—Bob Hope Special. NBC. Nov. 1994.
Woolf, Virginia. *A Room of One's Own*. New York: Harcourt Brace & Company, 1929.
Wollenburg, Skip. "Will the advertisers stay if "Ellen" says she is gay?" *The Denver Post* 23 Sept. 1996: 6G.
Yeats, William Butler. *The Collected Poems of William Butlter Yeats*. London: Macmillan & Co. Ltd., 1965.
The Young at Heart Comedians. Prod. Paramount Pictures. Videocassette #2386. Showtime, 1984.
Zoglin, Richard. "The Season of the Stand-ups." *Time*. 20 Sept. 1993: 78-9.

Index

A

Abbot, Kevin, 68
Abzug, Bella, 38
The Advocate, 96, 97
Allen, Gracie, 9, 23, 24; *see also* Burns and Allen
Allen, Steve, *Funny People*, 11
Allen, Tim, 125
Apte, Mahavdev E., 4
Arnold, Roseanne, *My Lives*, 55, 68
Arnold, Tom, 55, 59
Awards; *see also* each comedian
    Cho, Margaret, 115
    Clinton, Kate, 96, 98
    Diller, Phyllis, 19
    Goldberg, Whoopi, 105, 111
    Poundstone, Paula, 100
    Roseanne, 54–55
    Tomlin, Lily, 34–37
    Wagner, Jane, 35
Auslander, Philip, 60, 125

B

Barnes, Clive, 73, 74, 76
Barr, Roseanne
    awards, 54–55
    biography, 53–56, 62
    cultural impact, 53
    feminism, 51–54, 62–63,
    historical context, 51, 64–65
    influenced by
        Moms Mabley, 57
        "New Wave" comedians, 60

        Pryor, Richard, 60
        Tomlin, Lily, 60
    influence on others
        Cho, Margaret, 69
        DeGeneres, Ellen, 69
        leadership in women's comedy, 51, 53
    men in audience, 64
    persona, 51, 53, 56, 58, 59
    politics of *Roseanne!*, 61–62
    stand-up thoughts 58, 60, 68
    style of comedy
        aggressiveness, 57–59, 60-2
        insult humor, 54–57
        jokes, 53, 57, 58, 63, 67
    technique/craft
        delivery, economy of language, 67
        voice, 57
        writing comedy 61, 66–68
    themes, 51, 60, 68
        domestic arena, feminist critique, 53, 60, 66, 68
        women's experience, 60, 63, 68–69
        working class, 57–58, 62, 68–69
    works
        beginning stand-up, 54–55
        books
            Roseanne: My Life as a Woman, 55
            Roseanne: My Lives, 55, 68
        one woman shows
            The Roseanne Barr Show (HBO special), 57–59, 63–66
            Roseanne: Live from Trump Tower, 61, 62, 63, 67

sitcom: *Roseanne!* (1988-1996), 55–56, 61–62, 68; see also Ch. 4.
television
  cooking show: *Domestic Goddess*, 55
  talk show: *The Roseanne Show*, 55
  reality show: *The Real Roseanne Show*, 55
  theatre: *The Wizard of Oz*, 55_
Barreca, Regina, 4, 5, 6, 8
Beatts, Anne, 23, 94
Behar, Joy, 94
Benny, Jack, 18, 24
Berle, Milton, 24
Bernhard, Sandra, 91
Bishop, Joey, 21
Body presentation, beauty
  Bernhard, Sandra, 91
  Cho, Margaret, 117–118
  Clinton, Kate, 91
  DeGeneres, Ellen, 123
  Diller, Phyllis, 20, 22, 23, 25–26,
  Poundstone, Paula, 91, 103
  Roseanne, 54, 59–60, 68, 91
  Tomlin, Lily, 48, 50
Boosler, Elayne, 32, 129
Brice, Fanny, 10
Bristol, Claude, *The Magic of Believing*, 17
Brooks, Mel, 31
Brown, Nicole, 96
Brown, Rita Mae, 95
Bruce, Lenny and "New Wave" comedy, 2, 9, 11–13
Burns and Allen, 9, 24
Bush, George, 97
Butler, Brett, 125, 126

C

Caldwell, Sarah, 38
Carson, Johnny, 7, 55, 57
Case, Sue Ellen, 6, 91, 92
Cassandra, 74
Channing, Stockard, 7
Chisholm, Shirley, 38
Cho, Margaret
  biography, 113, 114
  style, comparisons and contrasts, 113–115
  techniques/craft, 118
  themes
    expectations for women's looks, 117–118
    feminism, 117–118
    gay life, 116
    voice to the marginalized, 116
    mother, 116
    personal as public, 115
    race, 116–117
  works
    book: *I'm the One That I Want*, 113
    concerts
      I'm the One That I Want, 113, 116, 117
      Notorious C.H.O., 113, 115, 116, 117, 118
    film: *Notorious C.H.O.*, 115,
    television appearances, 115
    sitcom: *All American Girl*, 113, 115
The Choices We Made: 25 Women and Men Speak Out about Abortion, 106
Chopin, Kate, *The Awakening*, 1, 95
Christian Coalition, 97, 103, 121
Clinton, Bill, 98
Clinton, Kate
  biography, 94–95
  historical perspective, 89, 92
  philosophy of comedy, 96, 99–100
  technique, 98–100
  themes
    education, 96
    politics, 94, 96–98
    lesbian culture, 98
    religion, 96, 97
  works
    books and essays
      Don't Get Me Started, 95, 96
      "Making Light: Some Notes on Feminist Humor," 89, 95
    comedy concerts
      Babes in Joyland, 96
      Comedy You Can Dance to, 96
      Correct Me if I'm Right, 96
      Out Is In, 96
      Read These Lips, 96, 97, 98
      Y2K8, 96
Clowns
  social function, 3, 10, 11, 21, 24
  Diller, Phyllis, 9, 19, 20, 21, 23
  Roseanne in contrast, 56
Collier, Denise and Kathleen Beckett, 22, 23, 25, 32
Comedy teams
  Abbott and Costello, 9
  Burns and Allen, 9

Index 147

Martin and Lewis, 9
Comic Relief, 59, 100, 103, 105, 106
Comic Relief III, 107
Cosby, Bill, 49
Coser, Rose, 76
Crabtree, Lotta, 10
Crystal, Billy, 100, 107
Cultural impact of women's comedy, 1–3, 127–129; *see also* individual comedians
    Barr, Roseanne, 2, 13, 56–60
    Cho, Margaret, 114–115
    Clinton, Kate, 2, 96–99
    DeGeneres, Ellen, 121, 122–123
    Diller, Phyllis
        as pioneer, 19–20, 22, 33
        as point of departure, 2, 3
    Goldberg, Whoopi, 2, 106–109
    Poundstone, Paula, 2, 102–103
    Tomlin/Wagner, 2, 13, 45, 50
Curtin, Jane, 125

D

Daly, Mary, 95
Dangerfield, Rodney, 9, 24
Day O'Connor, Sandra, 6
DeGeneres, Ellen
    awards, 114, 119
    biography, 113,119, 120
    coming out, 114, 119–120; *see also* in works, *The Beginning* concert
    contrast to Cho, 113–114
    Esalen Institute, 120
    family values controversy, 121
    gay issues, 114, 120, 121–123
    interviews
        Fresh Air with Terry Gross, 114
        Prime Time with Diane Sawyer, 120
        The Right Words at the Right Time, ed. Marlo Thomas, 120
    "A Phone Call to God," 119, 122
    "The Puppy Episode," 120
    rapport with audience, 124
    style, 122
    techniques/craft, 123, 124
    television guest appearances, 119
    themes
        apolitical stance, 114
        everyday subjects, 114
    Time cover, 119
    works

        book: *My Point. . . And I Do Have One*, 113
    concerts
        The Beginning (2000), 114, 121–123
        Here and Now (2003), 114, 123–124
    films
        Coneheads, 119
        Dr. Doolittle, 119
        EDtv, 119
        Finding Nemo, 119
    television sitcoms
        Ellen, 113
        The Ellen Show, 119
    television specials
        If These Walls Could Talk II, 119
        One Night Stand: Command Performances, 119
        Women of the Night, 119
Descartes, 92
Diamond, Elin, 6, 90
Diller, Phyllis
    biography, 17–19
    costumes, 22, 23, 24, 91
    domestic humor
        housewife humor, 17, 25, 27, 28, 30
        invented family, Fang, etc., 17, 25, 28
        women literary humorists, 20
    feminist criticism, 23
    historical perspective, 23–25, 31–32, 71
    Illya Dillya, piano concerts, 22
    influences, 9, 23, 24; *see also* Hope, Bob
    influence on others, 19, 31–32
    persona, 9, 19, 21–23, 29
    performance venues, early, 17, 18
    retirement from stand-up, 19
    style of comedy
        contrasted to Tomlin, 50
        husband jokes, 32; wife jokes, 24
        one-liners, 17, 20, 21–22, 29
    self-deprecation, 24, 32
    technique/craft of jokes and delivery, 20, 29–32
    works, 18–19
        books
            The Complete Mother, 18
            The Joys of Aging and How to Avoid Them, 18
            Phyllis Diller's Housekeeping Hints, 18
            Phyllis Diller's Marriage Manual, 18

film
   Boy Did I Get a Wrong Number, 18
   A Bug's Life, 18
   Eight on the Lam, 18
   Splendor in the Grass, 18
records
   Are You Ready for Phyllis Diller?, 17, 27, 30
   Born to Sing, 18
   Phyllis Diller Laughs, 26, 28, 30, 31
   What's Left of Phyllis Diller?, 27
television
   appearances on comedy and variety shows, 18, 23
   The Phyllis Diller Show, 18
   The Pruitts of Southampton, 18
theatre
   Hello, Dolly!, 19
   Nunsense, 19
Draper, Ruth, 48–49
The Drew Carey Show, 19
Dylan, Bob, 65

E

Esalen Institute, 120
Esquire, 69
Ethnicity, 115, 116–117

F

Falwell, Rev. Jerry, 121
Feminism
   Barr, Roseanne, 13, 58, 69
   Cho, Margaret, 97, 113, 117,
   Clinton, Kate, 94, 95, 101
   Goldberg, Whoopi, 104, 106
   historically in comedy, 65
   scholarship, 3–5
   The Search for Signs of Intelligent Life in the Universe, 73, 86, 87, 127
   Tomlin, Lily, 2, 38–39
   Tomlin/Wagner, 14, 36, 38 45, 50
Feminist humor vs. female humor, 4
Ferraro, Geraldine, 64
Fields, Totie, 32, 59
Fisher, Seymour and Rhoda, 21
French, Marilyn, 40, 73, 87
Friedan, Betty, *The Feminine Mystique*, 25
Fry, William, 129

G

Gaffney, Maureen, *The Kathy and Mo Show*, 6
Gandhi, Indira, 64
Gandhi, M., 102
Gates, Darryl, 108
The Gay and Lesbian Alliance against Defamation, 121
Gays and lesbians
   Cho, Margaret, 114, 116, 119
   Clinton, Kate, 95–96, 98–99, 128
   DeGeneres, Ellen, 119–123
   Roseanne, 57
   Tomlin/Wagner, 39
   The Search for Signs of Intelligent Life in the Universe, 72, 73, 82
   significance in comedy, 8, 15, 98, 99
The Geena Davis Show, 125
Glaspell, Susan, 95
Goldberg, Whoopi
   biography, 103, 104–105
   Dance Theatre Workshop in Manhattan, 104
   historical perspective, 103, 110–111
   name, "Whoopi," 104
   Nichols, Mike, 104, 111
   personal magnetism, 104, 111
   rejection of labels, 104, 106, 107
   San Diego Repertory Theatre, 104
   themes, 104, 106–109
      feminism, 104, 106
      poverty, 104, 106–107
      race, 104, 108–109
   technique/craft
      comedic possession, 110, 111
      compassion, 110–111
      shamanism, 110
   works:
      books and articles
         Book, 110;
         The Choices We Made: 25 Women and Men Speak Out About Abortion, 106
      documentary
         Beyond Tara, 107
         Unchained Memories, 107
      film
         The Color Purple, 105
         Ghost, 105
         Girl Interrupted, 105
         How Stella Got Her Groove Back, 105

The Lion King, 105
The Long Walk Home, 107
Sarafina!, 105
Sister Act, 105
one woman shows (Theatre)
  Moms, 104
  The Spook Show, 104
  Whoopi Goldberg, 104, 110
television
  quiz show: *Hollywood Squares*, 105
  series: *Star Trek: The Next Generation*, 105
  specials
    Academy Awards, 103
    Comic Relief, 103, 106–107
    Chez Whoopi (HBO special) 108
    Whoopi Goldberg: Direct From Broadway, 105
theatre (roles)
  A Funny Thing Happened on the Way to the Forum, 105
  early musical roles, 104
  Ma Rainey's Black Bottom, 105
Goodman, John, 62
Grasso, Ella, 38
Gregory, Dick, 12
Gross, Terry, *Fresh Air*, 114

H

Hall, Arsenio, 62, 115
Hart, Lynda, 6, 73
HBO specials
  DeGeneres, Ellen, 113, 114, 119, 121
  Goldberg, Whoopi, 15, 108, 109
  Poundstone, Paula, 100
  Roseanne, 55, 61, 67
  Tomlin, Lily, 36, 47
Heche, Ann, 99
Henley, Beth, 65
Henry III, William A., 75
Historical perspective of women's comedy, 1–3, 127–129; *see also* individual comedians.
Hope, Bob, 9, 18, 21, 24, 115
  Bob Hope's Overseas Christmas, 23
  Eight on the Lam, 18
Huffington, Arianna, 102
Hurston, Zora Neale, 95
Hymowitz, Carol and Michaele Weissman, 25, 27

I

Idealization of women, 4, 56, 68; *see also* Friedan, Betty
  Diller, Phyllis, 19, 20, 22, 25, 32
  Roseanne, 53, 56, 68
In the Life, 96

J

Jackson, Shirley, *Life among the Savages*, 20
Judge, Diane, 89

K

Kaplan, E. Ann, 91
Kaufman, Gloria, *Pulling Our Own Strings*, 4
Kerr, Jean, *Please Don't Eat the Daisies*, 20
King, Alan, 53
King, Billie Jean, 38
Kirby, E.T., 39, 74, 75
Kirkpatrick, Jean, 64
Kroll, Jack, 83

L

Lahr, John, 56–60
Lane, Nathan, 105, 106
Larry King Live, 121
Laugh-In, 34
Lawrence, Martin, 125
Levine, Emily, 9
Licensed spokesperson role,
  defined, 3
  Cho, Margaret, 116–118
  Diller, Phyllis, 24–28
  Goldberg, Whoopi, 106–109
  Roseanne, 60–65
  Tomlin, Lily, 38, 39, 50
  Wagner, Jane, 43–48
Liddy, Gordon, 77
Lin, Maya Ying, 65
Louis-Dreyfus, Julia, 125

M

Mabley, Moms, 58–59
Moms, 104
Moms Mabley on Stage, 58
MacDonald, Betty, *The Egg and I*, 20
"Male gaze," 91, 92
Mandela, Nelson, 122
The Mark Twain Award for Comedy, 37
May, Elaine, 9, 10, 44; *see also* Nichols and May

McClintock, Barbara, 65
McDaniel, Hattie, 107
McDonald, Betty, *Life Among the Savages*, 20
McPhee, Paul, 7
Meredith, James, 32
Michaels, Lorne, 50
Midler, Bette, 125
Mintz, Lawrence
    theories of stand-up, 3, 7, 9, 13
    negative exemplar and licensed spokesperson, 3, 39, 56, 76
Montgomery bus boycott, 107
Mother Jones, 100, 102
Ms. magazine, 82, 106, 117

N

The National Enquirer, 62
The National Film Board of Canada; see *Wisecracks*
The National Gay and Lesbian Task Force, 98
Negative exemplar role
    defined, 3
    Diller, Phyllis, 20–24
    Roseanne, 56–60
    Tomlin/Wagner, 39, 73
Newhart, Bob, 38
"New Wave" comedy, 2, 11–13
Nichols and May
    characters, 2
    funeral routine, 10–11
    historical impact, 11–13, 44
    satire, 44
    Tomlin's admiration, 39, 43
    techniques, 44
    works
        The Best of Nichols and May, 43
        An Evening with Nichols and May, 44
        Improvisations to Music, 43
Noble, Elaine, 38
Norman, Marsha, 65

O

Oedipus, 73
One woman shows (theatre)
    Whoopi Goldberg, 49
    Gilda Radner, 49
    Lily Tomlin, 71–72

P

Paar, Jack, 18
The Peabody Award, 35
The Penguin Book of Women's Humor, Barreca, 92, 94
Pentland, Bill, 54, 55
Piercey, Marge, 95
Pershing, Linda, 99
Political comedy
    Clinton, Kate, 95–98
    Goldberg, Whoopi, 106–109
    Poundstone, Paula, 94, 102–103
    Tomlin, Lily, 35, 36, 38
    Wagner, Jane, 77, 82
Political leaders, 97
Poundstone, Paula
    biography, 100–101
    contrasts to Phyllis Diller, 101
    historical perspective, 89
    Mother Jones, 100, 102
    rapport with audience, 102
    style, 100, 102
    themes
        domestic, 101
        political, 94, 102–103
The Progressive, 96
Pryor, Richard, 36, 37, 60, 114
    influence on Roseanne, 9
    work with Lily Tomlin, 48–49

Q

Quayle, Dan, 107

R

Radner, Gilda, 7, 8, 49
Rasmussen, Zora, 8
Reaganomics, 64, 73
Reich, Robert, 65
Reiner, Carl, 37
Rich, Adrienne, 95
Rich, Frank, 73, 76, 82, 87
Rickles, Don, 57
Ride, Sally, 65
The Right Words at the Right Time, 120
Rivers, Joan, 32, 42
Robertson, Pat, 97
Roe v. Wade, 38
Rogers, Will, 13
Roseanne; see Barr, Roseanne
The Rosie O'Donnell Show, 96, 100
Rosie the Riveter, 25
Rukeyser, Muriel, 95

Index

S

Saturday Night Live, 22, 23, 50, 119, 125
Sahl, Mort, 11
Schlafly, Phyllis, 64
Schlatter, George, 34
The Screen Actors Guild, 127
The Search for Signs of Intelligent Life in the Universe
   audience as collaborator, 75–76
   characters
      Agnus, 73, 77–79
      Mrs. Beasley, 73
      Brandi, 76, 77, 80–81
      Chrissy, 43, 76, 81
      Edie, 73, 86
      Ivan, 73
      Kate, 73, 81, 86, 87
      Lud, 73, 77, 80
      Lyn, 76, 84–85
      Marge, 77, 85
      Marie, 73, 80
      Pam, 75
      Paul, 73
      Tina, 76, 80, 6–88
      Trudy, 73–75, 77, 80, 86–88
   critical reaction, 73–74, 82–83, 87
   development, 75–76
   impact on women's comedy, 88
   performance transformations, 83, 84
   political and social commentary, 82, 87–88
   production, 72–73, 85
   shamanism as technique, 73–75, 77
   structure, 77
   themes, 72, 77, 82, 87–88
   Wagner, Jane; *see* Wagner, Jane
   women's movement, 82, 84, 86
Self-deprecation, 2
   Diller, Phyllis, 24, 32
   male comedians, 24
   Roseanne, 50
Seinfeld, Jerry, 115, 125, 126
Shakespeare
   Judith, 71
   King Lear, 3
   Hamlet, 1
Shamanism
   Goldberg, Whoopi, 110
   purpose in comedy, 128
   Tomlin, Lily, 39-40, 50
   Tomlin/Wagner, in *Search,* 74–75
Sheen, Martin, 125
Sheppard, Alice, 6
Shore, Mitzi, 54–55, 68
Sills, Beverly, 38
Simpson, O.J., 96
Snow, Carrie, 93
Spielberg, Stephen, 105
Stand-up
   challenges to women, 4, 6–7, 90
   history, 8, 15, 127–128
   pioneers, 13, 127; *see also* Phyllis Diller, Lily Tomlin, and Roseanne
   power for women performers, 8, 129
   role in society
      as clown, 3, 20, 128
      as revolutionary, 6, 8, 127–128
      for television , 125–127
      significance, 1-3, 127–128
      as social commentary, 8, 14
      use of female body, 22–23, 91
      use of women's themes, 90–94
Standing Up for Women
   Gaffney, Mo, 6
   Diller, Phyllis, 18, 23, 25, 30, 31
Stein, Gertrude, 66
Steinem, Gloria, 38
Stoddard, Karen, 23
Stone, Elizabeth, 40
Sullivan, Mort, 31

T

Technique of comedy
   Diller's one-liners, 21–22, 29–32
   Roseanne's insult humor, 54–57
   Tomlin's comedic possession, 39, 50
Television and comedians, 125–127
   1990s and changes in sitcom development, 125
   1996, a strong year for female stand-ups, 125
      Ellen, Ellen DeGeneres, 125
      Murphy Brown, Lily Tomlin, 125
      Roseanne!, Roseanne Barr, 125
   popularity of sitcoms featuring stand-up stars, 125
      Grace Under Fire, Brett Butler, 126
      Home Improvement, Tim Allen, 125
      Kate and Allie, Jane Curtin, 125
      Martin, Martin Lawrence, 125
      Roseanne!, Roseanne Barr, 125
      Seinfeld, Jerry Seinfeld, 125
      Third Rock from the Sun, Jane Curtin, 125
   quality of women's roles, 126
   reality TV and its effect on sitcoms, 127

sitcoms and comedians, 125–126
   The Bette Show, Bette Midler, 125
   Murphy Brown, Candace Bergen, Lily Tomlin, 126
   West Wing, Lily Tomlin, 125
women executives and women stars, 126
women's experience as sitcom subject, 126
Television shows of the '50s and '60s
   Father Knows Best, 28
   Leave It to Beaver, 27
   Make Room for Daddy, 28
   Ozzie and Harriet, 27
Thatcher, Margaret, 64
Thomas, Ben, 55
Thomas, Clarence, 108
Thomas, Dylan, 66
Thomas, Marlo, 106
Three Sisters, 126
The Today Show, 106
Tomlin, Lily
   awards, 34 37
   biography, 34–38
   characters
      Mrs. Beasley, 35, 40–41, 44
      Crystal, 36, 39, 45, 46–47
      Edith Ann, 34, 35
      Ernestine, 33, 34, 35, 44
      Glenna, 36
      Lud and Marie, 48
      Rick, 45
      Sister Boogie Woman, 39, 45, 47–48
      Suzie Sorority, 34, 40, 41, 44
      The Tasteful Lady, 34, 35
      Tess, 45, 46
   historical perspective, 38–39
   influences
      Bruce, Lenny, 39
      Draper, Ruth, 48–49
      Nichols and May, 39, 43–44
         The Best of Nichols and May, 43
         Improvisation to Music, 43
   influence on others, 38, 49–50
      Goldberg, Whoopi, 49
      Michaels, Lorne, 49
      Pryor, Richard, 48, 49
      Radner, Gilda, 49
      Roseanne, 50
   persona, 39
   style of comedy
      character comedy, 37, 48, 50
      satire, 33, 34, 36, 41
      technique/craft, 48–49: shamanism, comedic possession, 39–40, 50 themes: healing society, 40, 49–50; social justice, 43–48; social and political satire, 33–36, 41, 45
   works
      improvisation, 34
      records
         And That's the Truth, 34
         Ernestine: Peak Experiences, 33
         Modern Scream, 41–42
         This Is a Recording, 42
      television specials
         Lily, 35
         Lily Sold Out!, 35, 44, 72
         The Lily Tomlin Show, 35
      television variety shows
         The Flip Wilson Show, 35
         The Gary Moore Show, 34
         Laugh-In, 34
         The Merv Griffin Show, 34
      television character roles
         Murphy Brown, 37, 125
         The West Wing, 37
      theatre:
         Appearing Nitely!, 47–48, 72–74
         The Search for Signs of Intelligent Life in the Universe, 50, 78–88; *see also* Wagner, Jane
The Tonight Show, 55, 57, 100, 119
To Tell The Truth, 100
Truth, meaning in comedy, 90
Twain, Mark, 13
Tyler, Robin, 93
Tynan, Kenneth, 11, 13

V

The Vagina Monologues, 96
Vaid, Urvashi, 95
Vernon, Jackie, 11
The Village Voice, 98

W

Wagner, Jane, 50–51
   artistry described, 72
   playwright, *The Search for Signs of Intelligent Life in the Universe,* 71–73, 87–88
   writer for Lily Tomlin 34–37
Walker, Alice, *The Color Purple,* 105
Walker, Nancy, 4–6, 20, 71

Index

Ward, Artemeus, 13
Wasserstein, Wendy, *The Heidi Chronicles*, 65
Watergate, 77
Weisstein, Naomi, 25
West, Mae, 10
What About Joan?, 126
Wife jokes, 24; husband jokes, 32, 58
Wilde, Larry
    Diller, Phyllis, 23, 27, 29, 30, 31
    jokes, 14, 18, 20, 21, 24
    teams of comedians, 9
    writers, 29, 31
Williams, Matt, 62
Williams, Robin, 107
Wilson, August, *Ma Rainey's Black Bottom*, 105
Winer, Linda, 87
Winstead, Liz, 92
Winters, Jonathan, 38
Wisecracks
    Behar, Joy, 94
    jokes quoted, 93
    Poundstone, Paula, 101, 103
    power of comedy, 129
    women's bodies, 92
    women's vs. men's humor, 71
Womankind, 91, 100

Women's Movement
    Clinton, Kate, 95
    Conclusion, 95
    Diller, Phyllis, 31
    Overview, 2, 14
    Tomlin, Lily, 38–39
    The Search for Signs of Intelligent Life in the Universe, 82, 83, 84, 86
Woolf, Virginia, 68, 71
Working class, 57
Writing comedy, 61, 68; *see also* technique/craft for each comedian:
    Diller, Phyllis, 29–31
    Roseanne, 66–68
    Sullivan, Mort, 31

Y

Yeats, W. B., 84
Youngman, Henny, 11, 29, 57

DISCARDED